MURDER BY MILKSHAKE

MURDER BY MILKSHAKE

AN ASTONISHING TRUE STORY OF ADULTERY, ARSENIC, AND A CHARISMATIC KILLER

EVE LAZARUS

ARSENAL PULP PRESS
VANCOUVER

MURDER BY MILKSHAKE
Copyright © 2018 by Eve Lazarus

ARSENAL PULP PRESS
Suite 202 – 211 East Georgia St.
Vancouver, BC V6A 1Z6
Canada
arsenalpulp.com

The publisher gratefully acknowledges the support of the Canada Council for the Arts and the British Columbia Arts Council for its publishing program, and the Government of Canada, and the Government of British Columbia (through the Book Publishing Tax Credit Program), for its publishing activities.

Arsenal Pulp Press acknowledges the xʷməθkʷəy̓əm (Musqueam), Sḵwx̱wú7mesh (Squamish), and səl̓ilwətaʔɬ (Tsleil-Waututh) Nations, speakers of Hul'q'umi'num'/Halq'eméylem/hən̓q̓əmin̓əm̓ and custodians of the traditional, ancestral, and unceded territories where our office is located. We pay respect to their histories, traditions, and continuous living cultures and commit to accountability, respectful relations, and friendship.

Unless otherwise attributed, photos are courtesy of Jeannine Castellani-Waller.

Cover and text design by Oliver McPartlin
Edited by Susan Safyan
Copy edited by Shirarose Wilensky
Proofread by Alison Strobel

Printed and bound in Canada

Library and Archives Canada Cataloguing in Publication:
Lazarus, Eve, author
    Murder by milkshake : an astonishing true story of adultery, arsenic, and a charismatic killer / Eve Lazarus.

Issued in print and electronic formats.

ISBN 978-1-55152-746-8 (softcover).—ISBN 978-1-55152-747-5 (PDF)

    1. Castellani, Esther. 2. Castellani, Rene. 3. Murder—British Columbia—Vancouver. 4. Trials (Murder)—British Columbia—Vancouver.
I. Title.

HV6535.C33V35 2018   364.1'5230971133   C2018-904939-1
                                                       C2018-904940-5

For Mike, Mark, Megan, and Matthew
and for
Jeannine, Ashley, and Lindsay

CONTENTS

INTRODUCTION

I've had a fascination with the Castellani murder case since I first saw the true-crime exhibit at the Vancouver Police Museum in the 1990s. This crime had all the ingredients for a movie of the week: an adulterous middle-aged celebrity husband, who, rather than fight for divorce and face the wrath of the Roman Catholic Church, decided to poison his wife so that he could marry a twenty-five-year-old switchboard operator.

I've read various accounts of the murder over the years, even written about it myself in my book *At Home with History*, grounding the story in the house, or in this case, the duplex, where most of the poisoning took place. Occasionally, I've told the story on the radio, usually around Halloween, and then, in 2011, I wrote a post about it on my blog *Every Place Has a Story*.

The blog post changed everything, because, fortunately for me, I had made a mistake.

Debbie Miller emailed to tell me that Lolly, "the other woman," had a son called Don, not a daughter, as I had written. And Don—her husband—would very much like to find Jeannine, the Castellanis' daughter, because he'd been searching for her for nearly fifty years. I wrote back and thanked Debbie and said I would also like to find Jeannine.

And then, in June 2017, Jeannine found me.

She and her daughter Ashley came to my book launch for *Blood, Sweat, and Fear* at the Vancouver Police Museum. The museum had recently overhauled its true-crime exhibits and now had more detailed and sensitive coverage of the Castellani murder, featuring Esther instead of Rene, situated right next to our makeshift bar in the old autopsy suite where Esther had once lain.

I told Jeannine that Don had been looking for her, and she got quite emotional. She had also been searching for Don for nearly half a century.

So why write a book about what is already one of the most sensational and unbelievable murders in Vancouver's history?

Well, several reasons. It took place at a turning point in the 1960s—a decade of incredible change in Vancouver and elsewhere. On the one hand, you had conservative, small-town Vancouver and two juries that condemned Rene mostly because of his infidelity. On the other hand, you had free love and be-ins, hippies and the Beatles, and a seismic political, cultural, and legal shift happening all over North America.

It was the era of Mad Men, of gin breakfasts and martini lunches—and Rene Castellani may just have been the maddest ad man of them all.

It was a nineteenth-century–style murder solved by a twentieth-century doctor and old-fashioned police work.

And it was a time when the death sentence was still on the table.

But, most of all, I wanted to write this book to tell Jeannine's story.

Author's Note

With the exception of the taped interviews of Gloria Yusep, Esther's sister, by author Susan McNicoll in 2005 and 2006, the quotes from those directly involved in the Castellani murder case have come from police statements, the inquest, the preliminary hearing, and the two trials. I've made extensive use of newspaper clippings from the period for colour and conducted dozens of interviews with family members, friends of the family, and experts.

THE CAST

Esther Castellani (1925–1965)

    Mother: Mabel Henderson Luond

    Stepfather: Karl Luond

    Brother: Karl Jr., married to Sheila

    Sister: Gloria, married to Bud Foxgord (1948–1964)

        married to George Ridgeway (1963–1964)

        married to Elmer Yusep (1965–)

    Daughter: Jeannine (1953–)

    Granddaughters:

        Lindsay (1980–)

        Ashley (1984–)

Rene Castellani (1925–1982)

    Mother: Marie Castellani

    Father: Rene Castellani

    Sisters:

        Jeanne

        Louise

        Rose

Adelaide Ann Darwin ("Lolly") (1939–?)

    Husband: Donald Miller (1960–1962)

    Mother: Augie Giuliani

    Stepfather: Mario Giuliani

    Son: Donald Miller (1959–)

Iaci Family

Frank Iaci (senior)

Wife: Eva Iaci (1918–1962)

Sons:

Frank Jr.

Ross ("Jake")

Benito ("Benny")

Daughters:

Lucia ("Toots")

Rose ("Koko")

Marie Helen ("Teenie")

Brother: Joseph Iaci, married to Erma Iaci

Daughters:

Gloria

Josephine

CKNW Senior Staff, 1965

Bill Hughes: Station manager

Mel Cooper: General sales manager

Erm Fiorillo: Comptroller

Hal Davis: Program manager

Medical Personnel (in order of appearance)

Dr John Sector: General practitioner

Dr Bernard Moscovitch: Internal medicine specialist

Dr Richard Beck: Specialist in hematology

Dr David Percy Jones: Neurologist

Dr David Hardwick: Senior pathologist (VGH)

Dr Frank Anderson: Associate resident in pathology

Ted Fennell: City analyst

Alexander J. Beaton: Chemist

Eldon Rideout: Assistant city analyst

Norman Erickson: Biologist, Crime Detection Laboratory, Ontario

Glen McDonald: Judge and coroner

Dr Thomas Redo Harmon: Pathologist

Dr James Rigsby Foulkes: Head of the Department of Pharmacology at the University of British Columbia

Dr Harold Taylor: Head of pathology at Vancouver General Hospital

Lawyers

Samuel M. Toy: Prosecutor

Albert Mackoff: Defence lawyer, first trial

James Bartman: Magistrate

Stewart McMorran: City prosecutor

Charles Maclean: Defence lawyer, second trial

John Davies: Defence lawyer, second trial

Esther was buried at Forest Lawn Memorial Park
in Burnaby, BC, on July 14, 1965. (Courtesy Ashley
Waller, 2018)

PROLOGUE

On July 14, 1965, the family and friends of Esther Castellani gathered as she was buried at Forest Lawn Memorial Park in the Vancouver suburb of Burnaby, British Columbia.

The casket was a golden colour with silver handles, lined with gold-coloured silk. Inside, Esther was dressed in a powder-blue woollen suit and a white silk shirt that her eleven-year-old daughter, Jeannine, had chosen. In Esther's hands were her favourite lily of the valley flowers and a rosary.

Esther had been known as a happy, jolly woman who had made many friends during her forty years. They were all at her graveside ceremony—her boss, Joyce Dayton; her friend Frank Iaci; people from her husband's work at CKNW; and, of course, her family, with the exception of Jeannine, the Castellanis' daughter, and other children in the family, who were kept at home.

Earlier that day, the mourners had been to a service for Esther at a South Granville church, just outside Vancouver's downtown core. Her husband, Rene Castellani, stood outside the door. He wore dark glasses, chewed gum, greeted the mourners one by one, and then guided them through the doors as if they were going to see a performance—which, in a sense, they were. After the service, Rene handed out samples of Peter Jackson cigarettes—part of a CKNW promotion—to the smokers.

Esther's mother and father, Mabel and Karl Luond; sister, Gloria; brother, Karl Jr., and his wife, Sheila; and Rene climbed into a rented black limousine and rode to the cemetery—the lead car in front of a long line of mourners. As they drove along 12th Avenue, the limo became dangerously low on gas, and they had to back up to a gas station, with the hearse behind them, fill up, and continue on to the cemetery.

Esther's brother, Karl, shook his head and said, "Wouldn't Esther just crack up over this?"

Her father thought it was an omen.

Mabel and Karl Luond paid for the funeral and had their daughter buried in a plot they had arranged for themselves years before. There was a short graveside ceremony, and then Esther was lowered into the ground.

But Esther, who had suffered such a long, agonizing death, wasn't allowed to go that easily. Within a few weeks, she would be dug up and placed on a slab at the morgue while scientists searched for the cause of her death.

After she was reinterred, her parents couldn't bear to re-bury her under her married name, and so her headstone simply reads: *Esther Luond, mother of Jeannine.*

CHAPTER 1
ABUSIVE BEGINNINGS

Shortly after her daughter Esther was born in March 1925, Mabel Davis Henderson, twenty and unwed, moved from Calgary to Vancouver. There she met and married Karl Luond, a twenty-six-year-old Swiss baker. The wedding took place two days before Esther's second birthday. The girl was never told that Karl Luond was not her biological father.

Mabel was born in York, England, and listed Anglican as her religious denomination on the wedding certificate. Karl was Roman Catholic. They were married by Reverend Charles Williams at the Wesley Methodist Church in Vancouver's West End. Esther, Karl, and Gloria were brought up Catholic, and the girls attended St. Augustine's school in Vancouver's Kitsilano neighbourhood.

Luond was a short, angry man with a heavy Swiss accent who liked to gamble on the horses. During the Depression, he sold lemon buns and other baked goods door to door.

The Luonds' was a violent, unhappy home. Gloria told author Susan McNicoll in 2006 that she remembers her father and mother having terrible fights. One night, after a New Year's Eve party, when Gloria was about four, she saw her father hit her mother after the next-door neighbour kissed Mabel goodnight. "My father got very jealous, and he grabbed her by the hair and dragged her around," Gloria told McNicoll. "Afterward, my mother had her hair cut off and never wore it long again."

The children got the worst of it, though. One day, a nun at St. Augustine's phoned the Luonds and told them that Esther had been playing baseball with the boys in the schoolyard. When her father found out, he beat her so badly that he broke her nose and her arm. "My father had a very bad temper," said Gloria. "I was sitting at the table one time,

Esther, Karl, and Gloria Luond, circa 1930s.

and he just took the cat's bowl and smashed it across my face. We were not allowed to speak. When Dad would ask a question, if we answered, it was still talking back, and we weren't allowed to do that."

By the middle of the Depression, the family had moved above the bakery they operated. "My dad was very brutal. He just hit you whenever he felt like it," Gloria said. When she was fourteen, Gloria decided to skip school and look for a job. The school phoned her parents and Gloria got a beating. Gloria told McNicoll, and later, her niece, Jeannine, that although she and Karl got the worst of the beatings, Esther was sexually abused by her father. One night, when Gloria was about thirteen, she had been unable to sleep and came downstairs to the bakery. There she saw her eighteen-year-old sister with Karl on the table where the bread troughs were usually kept. "I'm sure he saw me, but I didn't say anything. I just went back to bed," said Gloria. Later, she took her mother aside

Esther and Gloria, circa 1940.

and told her what she had seen. "She brought Dad up from the bakery, and he hit me and said it wasn't true, that I was just making up stories."

Gloria told Susan McNicoll that her father was always making suggestive comments to her, and she would often lock herself in her bedroom. Although she was hit frequently, she wasn't sexually abused. "I never let him touch me. Couldn't stand him, and I couldn't stand my mother," she said.

When Karl was fourteen, said Gloria, and trying to defend himself from another beating, his father told him, "You're lucky I let you live with me," and then knocked the boy's head against the wall until he passed out.

In December 1944, Gloria's then boyfriend, a young man who played the violin and lived up the hill on 12th Avenue, gave her a Christmas present. On Christmas day, her mother told her to go up to his house

Esther in her St. Augustine's uniform, circa 1940.

and thank him. "I'd already given him his Christmas present, and I didn't want to go because my shoes had big holes in them." Gloria started to argue with her mother. "I guess I spoke a little loud, and my father came running in and he pushed me." The new blouse that she'd just got for Christmas that morning caught on a hook and ripped. Gloria never forgot that.

"I said, 'Goddamn you,'" Gloria told McNicoll. "Then he threw me down the hallway by the furnace, and he shoved his foot in my face. He knocked my teeth out, and he smashed my nose." When she came to she was covered in blood. "I went into their bedroom to apologize, and my mother just grabbed me and pulled me into the kitchen. With the blood from my face, she wrote on the white cupboards: 'Xmas 1944—I wish he killed you,'" she said. "Because, you see, I had already said that he had an affair with my sister, so I guess they were always angry with me."

Luond expected a lot from his children. Esther left school at fifteen and worked as a helper in the bakery, and Karl, who was four years younger, was also made to leave school at fifteen. Shortly after the war ended, the Luonds' bought a house on Burnaby Street in Vancouver's West End and opened a bakery on nearby Davie Street. Gloria was allowed to finish grade ten before she was taken out to work full time in the family business. When she was eighteen, she caught the eye of a young doctor named Bud Foxgord who frequented the bakery. She couldn't wait to get away from her family and married him soon afterward.

Rene Castellani's father—also named Rene (and pronounced *Ree-knee*)—was an Italian who met his French wife, Marie, in Montreal. They had three daughters—Jeanne, Louise, and Rose—and then a son. In 1930, when Rene Jr. was five, they moved to Vancouver. The family lived in an old wood-frame house across from the courthouse on Hornby Street and one house away from the current Hotel Vancouver, which was then being built and would take more than a decade to finish. The Castellani parents ran an Italian delicatessen on the spot now occupied by Robson Square, one of a cluster of little shops that provided food, clothes, and services to the Depression-era families of the West End.

Rene was a boy soprano with a beautiful clear voice, who sang at High Mass at the Holy Rosary Cathedral. He went to Vancouver College until he was sixteen and then moved with his parents to small-town Trail in southeastern BC in 1941. He helped out with the cooking in his parents' concession and got his first job in the lead burner section at the Consolidated Mining and Smelting Company of Canada. The

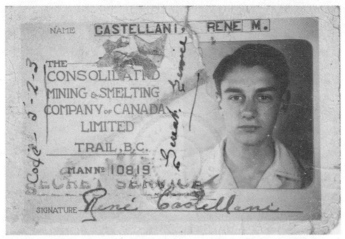

Rene's first job was in the lead burner section of the Consolidated Mining and Smelting Company of Canada in Trail, BC.

operation produced heavy water,"[1] which was used as a moderator in nuclear reactors. During World War II, the smelter was seconded to the Manhattan Project, the US, Canadian, and UK research undertaking responsible for producing the atomic bomb. The Trail smelter was known as Project 9. But Rene would not explode into Vancouver's criminal history until years later.

Jeannine kept her father's identity tag from the smelter with his picture and his signature on it. It is also stamped *Secret Service*—twice on the front and once on the back.

The back of the tag notes that Rene was transferred to Vancouver on January 2, 1943. Later that year, he joined the merchant navy and was soon wearing the navy-blue radio officer's uniform and charming the hostesses at the United Services Centre on Burrard Street—a recreation centre set up by the Rotary Club for men and women in the armed forces on leave in Vancouver. The food was decent and reasonably

---

1   Water in which the hydrogen in the molecules is partly or wholly replaced by the isotope deuterium.

Rene and Esther Castellani were married on July 16, 1946, at the Holy Rosary Cathedral.

priced, and there was a billiards room, as well as a Wurlitzer and a player piano for dancing to at night.

After his discharge from the navy, Rene worked at Washer Parts and Service on Richards Street in downtown Vancouver, started writing and acting in plays with a local theatre company, and made connections with future radio deejays Jack Cullen and Gerry Davies. He also reconnected with his childhood friend Frank Iaci. Frankie had studied at the Dayde Rutherford Dramatic Academy, become a child star in Los Angeles, and appeared as Willie on *Rambling 'Round Radio Row* in the early 1930s. Back in Vancouver, he performed in local productions at the Kitsilano Showboat and on radio under the name Frank James.

Frank's parents, Frank and Eva Iaci, lived at 1022 Seymour Street in Vancouver and ran a bootlegging joint out of their home—one of the few ways of making money during the Depression. Eva started making plates of pasta so her customers could have something to eat while they drank. Her food was so popular that soon she added to the menu, and the family home became a restaurant. Anything that

The Castellani wedding party at the Stanley Park Pavilion, July 16, 1946.

was left went to the hungry, who gathered at the back door. They got exactly what the paying customers got; Eva just asked that they bring a bowl. The Iacis named their restaurant the Casa Capri, the family called it 1022, and the locals just knew it as Iaci's. Rene spent a lot of time there, often working in the kitchen when they were short-handed.

And then he met twenty-one-year-old Esther Luond at a church function in 1946. He called her Es. After a short courtship, Esther and Rene were married at the Holy Rosary Cathedral on July 16, 1946. On the marriage licence, Rene's occupation is listed as general contractor, and Esther's is bakery helper. The witnesses were Frank Iaci Jr., and Esther's aunt Audrey Marie Henderson. Mabel threw them a big wedding reception at the Stanley Park Pavilion.

Esther and Rene lived with her parents after they married, first above the bakery, then in the West End. The young couple had financial problems from the start as Rene lurched from job to job. Nevertheless, "Esther was very happy with him," said Gloria. "He was a very funny guy." Gloria says their parents adored Rene, but she had reservations, and she and Esther would fight about him.

Frank Iaci and his family restaurant remained a big part of the Castellanis' lives. The restaurant was also a big part of Vancouver. It was the place to go for anyone looking for a good meal and a drink late at night. After performing at the Palomar or the Cave, stars such as Dean Martin, Milton Berle, Red Skelton, Tom Jones, Neil Sedaka, Louis Armstrong, Mitzi Gaynor, and Sonny and Cher would head to Iaci's, clutching an autographed photo made out to one of the family members—usually one of Frank's sisters, Koko, Teenie, or Toots. The framed photo would be nailed to the wall in the foyer, joining dozens of others. Situated at a distance from the city's nightlife and hotels, part of the restaurant's appeal was that it wasn't advertised or even legal, at least until 1963, when Eva bowed to pressure and took out a city licence.

Customers could park for free in the tiny lot in the back, go through the basement, climb up the stairs to the back porch, and then enter through the kitchen. Someone would be there to greet them, take their coats, and find them a seat in one of the three small front rooms, where they could check out the Iaci's old wedding photos or framed covers of *Life* and *Look* magazines. Or, if they preferred, guests could eat at a booth right in the kitchen while the family cooked and served around them.

Eva Iaci served up home-cooked meals with a bottle of Chianti and a side of pizza bread. The menu was simple—spaghetti with meat sauce or meatballs, a T-bone steak, ravioli, or chicken cacciatore. For dessert, there was usually spumoni ice cream, Eva's homemade cheesecake, or peach pie. A card clipped to the menu read, *Dear God. Please save us from the Italian man that expects us to cook as well as his mother. How in the hell can we when his wife can't?* The Iacis ran the

Joe Iaci and Rene Castellani on Granville Street, circa 1946.

restaurant for fifty years. In 2005, they were posthumously inducted into the BC Restaurant Hall of Fame.

Before Frank Jr.'s niece Gloria (Iaci) Cameron moved to Campbell River with her family in the late 1940s, she lived next door to her cousins on Seymour Street and remembers Rene and Esther well. Gloria spent a lot of time at Iaci's restaurant, helping her aunt Eva in the kitchen and watching her work. "I remember her sitting downstairs in the basement kitchen, and she would peel every mushroom because that was the way they should be." The Castellanis would often take Gloria out with them. Esther, she says, was very kind. "Esther was just a happy person. I always remember her for that, and [for her] really hearty laugh," says Cameron. "I remember as a little girl being very comfortable with them both. They were young and they treated me well."

She remembers Rene taught her skits and acted like Red Skelton.

"Whenever there was a get-together of people, he and Frank would perform and entertain. The two of them reminded me of Jerry Lewis and Dean Martin—they had that kind of banter going on."

Frank's brother Joe Iaci and his wife, Erma, lived next door to Casa Capri on Seymour Street. Joe was the owner of Kandid Kamera Snaps, one of the first street photography businesses in Vancouver. During the Depression, when there was little money for studio portraits, photographers snapped photos of people walking down the street—usually Granville or Hastings Street. The photographer handed the person a numbered ticket and invited them to drop by their shop later that day to buy a copy of the photo.

One of Joe's first hires in 1934 was a twenty-year-old Italian named Foncie Pulice. Pulice was finding that job opportunities were limited for Italian Canadians, and his job as a house painter didn't match his outgoing personality. When Pulice joined Kandid Kamera, Joe paid him forty cents for every 100 photos—and Pulice averaged about 1,500 a day. Their work grew during the war years, with servicemen who wanted photos to send home or take with them to the front. Pulice worked for Kandid Kamera until 1943, when he left to serve in the Canadian Armed Forces. When he returned to Vancouver, he found that Joe had bought into the Willows Hotel in Campbell River and was moving his family to Vancouver Island. Foncie hung out his own shingle in 1946 and called his company Foncie's Fotos.

There were several street photographers working in Vancouver in the late 1940s, and by 1948, one of them was Rene Castellani—listed in the city directory as proprietor of Rene's Photos. Rene had worked briefly for Joe Iaci, helping to develop photos in Joe's Seymour Street basement, and he was a natural salesman.

He and Esther moved out of the Luonds' home and into a house across the road, in the same building that his parents-in-law were

Jeannine Castellani, about age six, outside 232 East 22nd Avenue,
late 1950s.

married in more than two decades before. The church had been
converted into an apartment building during the war.

But Rene's photography business was short-lived. In 1950, he and
Esther moved to Kitsilano, and Rene went back to work as a washing
machine repairman—a job he'd held at the end of the war. Esther
had left her family's Alpine Bakery and worked at Cordell, a women's
wear company with retail stores on Hastings and Granville streets.
By the time Jeannine was born in November 1953, Rene had burned
through a series of jobs—mostly warehouse and maintenance—and
the Castellanis were living in a Craftsman-style house in Vancouver's
Mount Pleasant neighbourhood.

Jeannine's first memory is from the next house they rented, in
1956. It was a smart-looking California bungalow at Mount Pleasant's
Main Street and East 22nd Avenue. She remembers the school bus

picking her up and taking her to Little Flower Academy and bringing her home again, because her mother didn't drive.

The Castellanis lived in that house for four years, and Jeannine has a lot of good memories of their life there. "I remember watching *The Ed Sullivan Show* on Sunday nights," she says. "We'd watch that, my dad and I, and I would brush my dad's hair, even though he had a crew cut. We would sit in the living room and Mum cooked in the kitchen—it seemed like a pretty normal family." Rene made Jeannine cribs for her dolls. "My dad was really talented. He could play music on the piano by ear, he could sing, he could paint, he could act." Jeannine remembers that they rented out the attic of their house to an upholsterer named Stan, which provided the family with extra income. "After that house, we moved a lot."

The family's moves are laid out in the city directories. They lived in the East 22nd Avenue house until 1960, when Rene became manager of his brother-in-law's start-up company, Hydro Pure Sales. That year, Esther's father loaned them the money for a down payment on their own house at 2066 West 42nd in the middle-class area of Kerrisdale. Now Jeannine and Esther could walk to the Kerrisdale Community Centre, where Jeannine took swimming lessons. And they started to settle into the new place.

"It was a really nice older house, and we had a lot of good times there," says Jeannine. "I would go smelt fishing with my dad at Spanish Banks [a beach in Vancouver's West Point Grey neighbourhood]. My mum would come sometimes, sometimes not. My dad was goofy. Seals would come and get the smelts, and he'd imitate the seals. I remember really happy times. Then we had to move again."

Rene's latest get-rich scheme was a disaster. They lost the house, Karl lost his down payment, and the Castellani family moved into a cramped apartment above a hairdressing salon nearby.

In the early 1950s, Esther worked as a saleswoman at Cordell, a
women's wear store on Granville Street.

CHAPTER 2
THE WILLOWS

On April 2, 1961, Joe Iaci died from the leukemia that he'd been fighting for the past two years. He left a little more than $200,000 to his wife Erma and $100 a month for his mother, Rose. The balance of his estate was split between his daughters, Gloria and Josephine. The running of the Willows Hotel in Campbell River went to his nephew Frank Iaci and his friend Rene Castellani.

Campbell River was a fishing and logging town on the east coast of Vancouver Island. It wasn't the kind of place that appealed to a city boy like Rene, and Esther refused to take Jeannine out of Little Flower Academy or move away from her family and friends—even if it meant living above the Dora Day Beauty Salon. But Rene didn't have much choice. The Hydro Pure filtration system had failed to sell, and once again, he was broke.

"After my dad died, Frank and Rene came up to help my mother run the hotel, and in those days this town was isolated and tiny," says Gloria (Iaci) Cameron. "There were maybe one or two grocery stores and a couple of hotels. Campbell River was just a very sleepy town they called the Gulch."

The original Willows Hotel had opened in 1904. Four years later, a second Willows Hotel was built on Island Highway a few blocks south, and the original hotel was renamed the Annex. In 1909, one person died when the hotel burned down. A third Willows Hotel was rebuilt in its ashes.

Joe Iaci had headed a group that bought the Willows Hotel in 1948. The sixty-room hotel was the social centre of the town. There was a beer parlour, coffee shop, and lounge with a wide-open parlour

Sheila and Susie Luond with Esther and Jeannine
Castellani, getting ready for a fashion show at Joyce
Dayton's second children's wear boutique in Park Royal,
circa 1963.

and big easy chairs. Joe lived next door in the Iaci Block, became
a Rotarian, and hosted the Rotary Club at his hotel. The board of
trade, Toastmasters, United Fishermen and Allied Workers' Union,
and the school board all held their meetings at the Willows.

Esther decided to look for a part-time job now that Jeannine
was nine and more independent. She quickly found a sales position
with Joyce Dayton, who had just opened a children's boutique in
Kerrisdale within walking distance from their home. The two women
immediately clicked—they were close in age, became good friends,
and often went out together socially. Asked to describe Esther, Dayton
said, "She was a nice, big, bouncy, and jolly woman who was liked
by everyone."

Esther was hired full time at the store in May 1962. Shortly after,
Esther and Jeannine were able to move out of the cramped apartment
over the hairdressers' and into a duplex on West 42nd, on the same

Jeannine, with Rene as Santa Claus, at Joyce Dayton's
store, circa 1963.

block as the house that Esther's father had helped them buy just a
few years before. Esther could crank up her favourite Nat King Cole
records, and Jeannine was now old enough to ride her bike to Little
Flower Academy.

One morning, Esther took their little Pekingese/spaniel mutt
to work with her, as she did every day, but on this morning, Lady
took off and was hit by a car as they were crossing West Boulevard.
Esther was devastated and knew Jeannine would be upset. To soften
the blow, Esther asked Gloria, who had always had poodles, to find
Jeannine a puppy. "My aunt was waiting at the back of Joyce Dayton
when I rode my bike from Little Flower," recalls Jeannine. "She had a
little ball of fluff. And Mum had been crying, and I knew something
had happened. She felt so bad because she had been walking Lady,
but she wasn't on a leash."

Jeannine named the little brown dog Cocoa.

Rene left Campbell River every weekend to see his family in Vancouver. The sleepy small town wasn't Rene's first choice, but hotel life fit him perfectly. Frank Iaci recalled that "Rene could fix anything, do anything. He was outgoing, loveable, and never had an enemy in the world."[2] Gloria Cameron remembers him as "a very good person in Campbell River. He would help people—fix their wiring" and contribute to the community. That first year, Rene played Santa Claus at the Campbell River Rotary Club Christmas party. And he made friends with the local constabulary.

William Mathison joined the Campbell River RCMP detachment that Christmas and met Rene soon after. "He tried to be friends with members of the RCMP, as he liked us to respond when he called for assistance," he said in an email to author Susan McNicoll in 2008. "He was a good source of information as to who was in town or if a person we were seeking had been in the hotel." Mathison said that he suspected that Rene played both sides of the fence. "Some people were told by him that we had been asking about them and were given the heads-up by Rene."

Gloria Cameron's husband was a bartender at the Willows Hotel, and the couple were good friends with Rene and Esther. "Mum and I went to Campbell River a couple of times," says Jeannine. "The hotel was very old and actually kind of cool." Cameron remembers babysitting Jeannine so that Esther and Rene could have some time alone. Once, the Castellanis looked after the Camerons' house and two small daughters while they took a holiday; other times, they stayed at the hotel.

Jeannine still has one of the letters that her dad wrote to her and her mother from Campbell River. It's typed on a piece of Willows Hotel stationery and dated July 15, 1962.

2   Chuck Davis, *Top Dog! A History of CKNW, BC's Most Listened to Radio Station* (Vancouver: Canada Wide Magazines Ltd., 1993), 80.

Dear Es: It won't be long now and my girls will be here at Gopher
Gulch. And I mean Gulch. Today the goddam pipe broke on
the first floor and then Frank took off with a mop and then I
took off with a pipe wrench and some pipes and then we fixed
it. Then as if that wasn't it, then came more water and off we
went again but this time we put in our resignations and took
a job at the funny farm. We have more stories to tell you and
will keep you in stitches for hours.

The second half of the letter becomes more serious as Rene hints
at some business venture that he and Frank were planning in Victoria.

Just think, in Victoria, people again, bright lights and one and
a half hours from Vancouver. Then I can spend a week at home
every two. You'll be nuts on what we have planned and it can't
miss. The nice thing, it won't cost too much money and best of
all I will be with my family. I will be like a travelling salesman
and when it is my week to work then over you and Jeannine
come on weekends.

Whatever the planned business was in Victoria—probably a hotel
or restaurant—it must have fallen through, either because of lack of
funds or perhaps because Esther had had enough.

And then, on Saturday, January 19, 1963, the Willows Hotel burned
to a heap of ashes and rubble. Four people died and thirty-eight locals
lost their jobs in less than two hours.

Rene was in Vancouver for the weekend, and Frank had left the
hotel at about 12:30 a.m. He was called back just after three a.m. to
find the hotel already engulfed in flames and guests fleeing the fire.
Some climbed down a metal fire escape at the front of the hotel, some

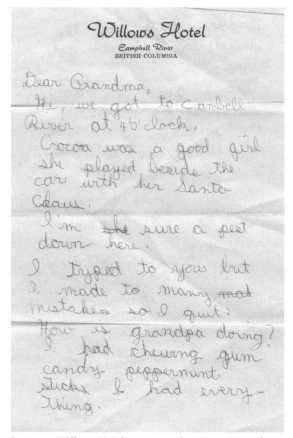

Letter on Willows Hotel stationery from Jeannine to her grandmother, 1962.

slid down planks extended from the second-floor roof, and others were plucked from windows by volunteer firefighters. Many were hurt as they leapt from windows. One hotel guest ran naked into the street in his escape from the fire. Another man suffered a fractured pelvis and broken ankle and ribs when, unable to reach a fire escape, he tried to slither down a drainpipe, which broke, dropping him ten feet (three metres) to the ground. Three men suffering fractures and burns to their arms and faces were taken to the hospital and treated by candlelight and flashlights because hospital power was knocked out by the fire.

The top floor of the hotel quickly caved in, and the walls finally collapsed around four a.m.; the only thing left standing was the smouldering chimney. The fire also destroyed a barber shop and a taxi stand, but firefighters were able to save the adjoining Iaci Block, which was separated from the hotel by a concrete wall.

The hotel register was burned in the fire, so there was some confusion about the precise number of guests staying in the hotel and their identities. It wasn't until the next day that searchers found three bodies so badly burned that they had to be identified by dental records, an eyeglass case, and a laundry label on a piece of clothing. The men were loggers from the area: Gerald (Gerry) Heenan, Charles Knudson, and Sven Lindgren. The fourth man, found a few days later, was David Johnson Lowe, a carpenter.

It took two days for the hotel's safe to cool enough to be opened. But when it was, the contents, which included a large sum of money, were all found intact.

Although the cause of the fire was never satisfactorily determined— faulty wiring or a cigarette left burning—arson was ruled out early on, as neither police nor the fire department officials found any evidence of oil or gasoline odours from the flames.

At the inquest, Fire Chief Oscar Thulin (whose great-uncle Charles Thulin built all three Willow Hotels) said that he had always anticipated the possibility of a large fire at the Willows. There had been about fifty minor fires at the hotel over the past twenty years, and the majority of them had been started by a cigarette dropped on bedding. Thulin told the jury he had made recommendations to the hotel management over the years—some had been carried out, and some hadn't. The hotel, he said, was used regularly by volunteer firefighters in their practice drills. Even so, he said, he had no idea the fire would spread as quickly as it did. The coroner's jury heard evidence that two of the hotel's wiring circuits were antiquated and not up to provincial standards. Staff had not been

Frank Iaci, manager, and Rene Castellani, assistant manager, at the Willows Hotel in Campbell River, 1962.

properly prepared in what to do in the event of a fire, and one of the fire escape exits had to be made through a linen storage room that was kept locked to avoid theft.

Frank Iaci told the inquest that the hotel had been in good shape financially at the time of the fire and later estimated the damage at about $250,000, the majority of which was not covered by insurance.

The loss of the hotel put Rene out of a job, and it left a huge gap in the town. On January 23, 1962, just four days after the fire, Frank Iaci gave an interview to the *Campbell River Courier*, saying that the major concerns for himself and his partner, Rene, were the staff. "This is a bad time of year for them to be out of work. What will they do? I honestly believe we had the happiest staff in the whole town." Frank said the hotel had been "home base" for many of the loggers and fishermen who worked in the area. "The lounge was their living room, where they met their friends, often where they found their next job," he said. "We knew so many of the customers, and a lot of them depended on us for help. We carried them over to the next pay day. Who is going to look after them now?"

Like his uncle Joe, Frank was active in the town. He joined the Rotary Club, gave talks, and, the year before the fire, had held a public art show in the hotel's dining room. "We had so many plans," he told the reporter. "When Rene and I first came here, we both thought that people who would sit in a boat for hours were crazy, but last summer the fishing bug hit us. When I caught my first salmon, that was it. But where are all those people from Quadra [Island] going to sit now? The lobby used to be full of them on Saturday nights."

Rene may not have been an arsonist, but he was definitely an opportunist. And he managed to make the best of the leftovers from the fire.

Jeannine has a clear recollection of when her father moved back to Vancouver. "I'm looking out the dining-room window, and I went, 'Mum, Dad's home and he's got a new car!' It was Gerry's car." (Gerry Heenan was one of the men who died in the fire.) Jeannine says he also brought home a big pile of silver coins that had melted together in the fire. "I remember him telling me the phone had melted."

She also recalls a picture that Rene painted of the Willows Hotel: "I wish I still had it. There were flames coming out of the Tudor windows and the outline of the three people who died. Their faces went from light flames to darker flames."

Dr Heather Burke, a forensic psychologist, says that although she understands that arson was ruled out as the cause of the fire, and Rene was in Vancouver at the time, she finds the painting revealing and disturbing; to paint people burning in a fire is an odd way to process grief. "People usually like to remember things in a positive way," she says. "He's artistically exploiting a tragedy. This isn't typical behaviour for someone grieving, and it makes me wonder if he had something to do with it."

The loss of his job meant that Rene could leave small-town life and return to Vancouver.

CKNW radio news commentator Jack Webster was called in by Warden Tom Hall to act as a go-between in the BC Penitentiary riot of 1963. (Photo by Ken Oakes, courtesy *Vancouver Sun*, April 26, 1963)

CHAPTER 3
THE MAHARAJA

By the early 1960s, the newer medium of television had begun to eclipse the popularity of radio, but its effect was minimized at CKNW. The performance of the New Westminster, BC, radio station was now so solid, and they had such an effective staff, that even this powerful entertainment force didn't slow it down. "Television started to get strong in the '50s, and people predicted the death of radio, but it didn't happen—it grew," says George Garrett, a news reporter who spent more than four decades at CKNW. "We were the most promotion-minded station you could imagine."

In 1957, CKNW hired Jack Webster, a crusty Scottish reporter who had immigrated to Canada after World War II and worked first at the *Vancouver Sun* newspaper and then took his hard-hitting reporting style to station CJOR, where he pioneered talk radio. Webster made his name after his daily reporting on the Mulligan police corruption scandal in 1955 but returned to Glasgow shortly afterward with his family. When CKNW offered the media celebrity double the salary he'd received at the competition and threw in a company car, Webster returned to Vancouver.

CKNW's investment in Webster really paid off in April 1963, when prisoners staged a full-scale riot and hostage-taking at the BC Penitentiary. Tom Hall, warden of the penitentiary, phoned Webster at home. Hall told Webster there were prisoners who wouldn't go back into their cells. "They want to speak to Prime Minister Pearson or Webster. We can't get Lester Pearson so we're calling you."[3] Webster

---

3   Jack Webster, *Webster! An Autobiography* (Vancouver: Douglas & McIntyre, 1990), 75.

alerted CKNW, picked up his tape recorder, headed for the penitentiary, and interviewed the prisoners, eventually negotiating the release of a prison guard.

CJOR fought back, hiring a stable of talk show hosts and pulling in thousands of new listeners. Their undisputed star was Pat Burns, who hosted a wildly popular phone-in radio talk show called the *Burns Hot Line*. His corrosive and angry show was pulling down such high ratings, CKNW began to pursue him, adding more money to its offer every time they talked. Burns refused to budge. Instead, CKNW doubled Webster's salary, gave him his own talk show—an investigative program called *City Mike*—let him broadcast from a studio in the Hotel Georgia, and left him to battle Burns for ratings.

CKNW's problems came to an end in August 1965, when Burns got the boot from CJOR and took a job with a Montreal talk radio station. Fans packed Vancouver's Queen Elizabeth Theatre for his farewell. The rental of the theatre was paid for by CKNW. "We were so happy to get him out of town," said Hal Davis, program manager.[4]

Radio was personality driven and, then as now, relied on advertising. That meant stations actively pursued listeners and ratings, and CKNW was one of the best. The station's promotions department continually thought up over-the-top promotions and stunts to get people talking about the station. In those days, the on-air talent, the copywriters, the salespeople, and the promotions staff were closely allied.

Before he became a familiar face as the funny weatherman with the many voices on the six p.m. news, Norm Grohmann began his radio career in 1954 and joined CKNW in 1961. Not long after he started with CKNW, Grohmann was approached by one of the promotions guys and asked if he had a radio in his car. He said he did. "Then they

---

4   Davis, *Top Dog!*, 74.

Rene Castellani and Jack Cullen, 1964. (Courtesy Colleen Hardwick)

went around and interviewed all the staff and found out that thirty-odd people had them. Then they were able to legitimately say that CKNW was first with the news with thirty two radio-equipped cars in the greater Vancouver area. Sure, they were radio equipped; they just had nothing to do with reporting news, but it sounded impressive."

CKNW was also one of the first stations to put news cruisers on the ground so that they could quickly be at the scene of whatever was making news that day—a fire, a shooting, or an accident. "CKNW had two news cruisers on the road with the CKNW logo on the side, and they numbered them three and four. No other station had a car on the road, and everybody thought CKNW had four of them," says Grohmann.

"Sponsors paid for everything, that's the way it worked," says Garrett. "I used to drive the first sponsored news cruiser. There was a loaf of Sunbeam Bread on each side of the station wagon, plus the Top Dog logo, the words CKNW in large letters, and the frequency, which was 1320 on the dial." Sponsored promotions were short, usually lasting a week or two at most. "It was hit 'em hard, hit 'em big, and hit 'em fast, and then get out of town," says Grohmann. "There could be a sonic boom or an earthquake that was 5.5 on the Richter scale and the ground actually shaking, and because CKNW was so well known for their promotions, some wag would say, 'It's probably just another CKNW promotion.'"

Rene Castellani and Jack Cullen had been radio operators in the Canadian navy during the war. Afterward, when Rene went back to fixing washing machines, Cullen enrolled in the Sprott-Shaw School of Commerce and Radio in Vancouver and landed a job with CKMO radio. Soon, he had his own gig—a midnight to dawn show called *Pacific Patrol*. Cullen turned it into an all-night party with his friends and their friends and was fired after the station janitor found a stash of beer on the fire escape. He spent six months in exile at CJAV in Port Alberni, returned to CKMO in the fall of 1947, and took over a late-night show called the *DX Prowl* from Frank Iaci. Iaci renamed it *The Owl Prowl*, and Cullen hosted the show, played his own records, and sold the ads. It was a huge hit, and CKNW poached Cullen and his show in 1949.

By the early 1960s, Cullen was one of a handful of deejays who had gained a following and celebrity status in the city. "He was the irreverent rebel in radio," said radio personality Red Robinson. "When I was a kid in the '50s, it was: 'Ladies and gentlemen, here is Doris Day.' Radio was formal. At one point at the BBC, they even used to read the news in a tuxedo."[5]

CKNW station manager Bill Hughes later told the *Vancouver Sun*'s John Mackie that he was constantly sending apologies for Cullen's

---

5   John Mackie, "Vancouver Loved Going to Bed with Jack Cullen," *Van-couver Sun*, April 29, 2002.

antics to the federal broadcasting commission in Ottawa. The straitlaced Vancouver of the 1950s had never seen anyone like Jack Cullen. He turned broadcasting on its head. Instead of doing the usual tightly scripted performances, he ad libbed virtually everything and was willing to go to any length to increase ratings. He did his show from a taxi, did weather forecasts by taking his mike to the roof of his studio, and broadcast from the gondola at Grouse Mountain while drinking hot rum. He dressed up as the Easter bunny, hopped all over town, and gave out prizes to whoever caught him. Audiences loved his stunts and unscripted shows, and *Vancouver Sun* columnist Jack Wasserman wrote of him, "Jack Cullen's ratings are so high not even his bosses believe it."[6]

Although CKNW headquarters was in New Westminster, Cullen broadcast out of different downtown Vancouver studios. One was over the Danceland Ballroom at Robson and Howe. Another studio was upstairs in an old Vancouver house. After six p.m., the only way to get into the studio was to climb up the outside of the house, over a wooden balcony, and through the window. A bottle of rum was the price of admission. *Province* columnist Bruce McLean wrote, "Cullen's studio looked like the waiting room at a detox centre."[7]

"Cullen was a night owl," recalls Norm Grohmann. "When he was working, it was always an open house—you'd go up and bring a bottle and you could sit around and watch Jack work and party. Rene Castellani was a good friend of Jack Cullen, and he used to go up and visit." Other regulars included newspaper columnists Jack Wasserman and Denny Boyd, singer Bobby Hughes, and Frank Iaci.

In 1961, Rene invented a character called Klatu from Outer Space with a strangely high-pitched voice. Klatu and Cullen would do different

---

6   Quoted in Davis, *Top Dog!*, 33.

7   Quoted in Davis, *Top Dog!*, 33.

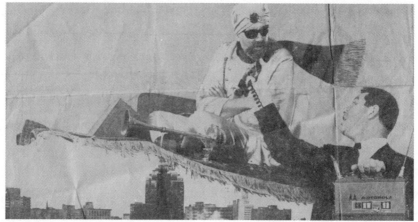

Rene Castellani as the Maharaja of Alleebaba, one of CKNW's most memorable promotions, October 1963.

routines on air. In one, Klatu tells Cullen: "I was over the Burrard Inlet and I ran out of gas. This is not normal because normally I have enough gas—you must have let it out, didn't you? Tell me now or I'll remove your nose." They sing a couple of songs together, and Cullen has Rene perform a crazy laugh in the echo chamber.

In another skit, disturbing in hindsight, Rene says: "Now, listen, dear. Now that your cage is cleaned, you can go back."

Unidentified female voice: "Did you drink all the DDT?"

Rene: "Oh, I left some for you, dear."

Unidentified female voice: "Oh, I'm glad. Thanks awfully for the cyanide."

In the fall of 1963, CKNW was going through a dip in the ratings, and the station needed something that would get them back on top.

After his work in the studio with Cullen and his stand-up comedy routines at different clubs around town, Rene was the obvious choice. Tony Antonias, the creative director at CKNW who is fondly remembered for coming up with the famous Woodward's $1.49 Day jingle and whistle in 1958, says he remembers being called into a meeting in the early 1960s with Mel Cooper, sales manager, and Hal Davis, program manager, in which they discussed doing a promotion with someone dressed up as a rich Indian prince who was coming over to buy the entire province of BC. "I came up with the title the 'Maharaja of Alleebaba,' and everybody said, 'Hey, I think we've hit on something,'" said Antonias.

"They got a Rolls Royce from somebody—maybe Jim Pattison—and Rene Castellani dressed up as an Indian potentate," says Grohmann. "He had on a silk outfit—pants and a jacket and a turban. I don't know if he darkened his skin—he was quite swarthy anyway—and he rode around in this limo. At predetermined times, a reporter named Shervin Shragge would interview him." The station took out billboards around the city featuring a picture of Rene as the Maharaja, and Shragge would give updates on the air about his supposed business dealings.

"Shervin would say, 'We have caught up with the Maharaja now and he is just entering the Hotel Vancouver. Excuse me, can I have a word with you?'" says Grohmann. "'Certainly, Mr Snag, Mr Shragge.' Rene would always call him the wrong name, anything that rhymed with Shragge—brag, hag, dag—you name it, and they had this little ping-pong game where he would say, 'Certainly, Mr Flag, Shragge, yes. I'm going to do this and I'm going to do that.'"

The station registered Rene at the Bayshore hotel (now known as the Westin Bayshore) as Maharaja Alleebaba and made sure he was always dressed in fancy costumes and surrounded by hired models dressed as dancing girls. At this time the Bayshore was very brand new—a top-of-the-line hotel with all the modern amenities. He and his entourage would visit the Cave nightclub, and Rene would pick up the tab for every table around him. "Everybody in town was talking about it," says Grohmann.

NO COMMENT, SAYS NEGOTIATOR. Despite strong denials from unofficial sources, rumours persisted today that B.C. had already been sold to the bearded buyer from the East, the Maharajah of Alleebaba. Seen here with an unidentified member of the negotiating committee, the Maharajah will reveal his firm purchase price today exclusively over radio CKNW-98.

Rene Castellani was supposedly so successful in his role as the Maharaja of Alleebaba that listeners to CKNW took to the streets with signs that read, *Keep BC British*, October 1963.

Photos in local newspapers showed Rene as the Maharaja of Alleebaba going to the houses of CKNW listeners who phoned in with answers to silly questions as part of an on-air promotion. "The moneyed Maharaja is now on an all-out program of house calls throughout Vancouver to meet the people and empty his treasury. Only CKNW has the details—and the money winning answers," went the promotion.

Another newspaper clipping shows a man costumed as an underling holding an umbrella over the Maharaja and on the other side a man "from the negotiating team" holding his hand over his face as he clutches a briefcase. "Rumours persisted today that BC had already been sold to the bearded buyer from the East," says the caption. "The Maharaja will reveal his firm purchase price today exclusively over CKNW." Supposedly Castellani was so convincing in his role that some locals took to the streets with signs reading, *Keep BC British*. Of course, they could also have been CKNW staffers in disguise.

The last newspaper photo has a picture of Castellani as the Maharaja sitting on a flying carpet superimposed over the city of Vancouver. He's wearing his trademark dark glasses and turban and being interviewed by the CKNW news reporter. In the final moments of his Vancouver tour, the Maharaja of Alleebaba says goodbye to the province that was not for sale. "It was fun trying to buy BC," he says. "It was fun to meet people, to reward their knowledge of this wonderful province, to test their reactions to my offbeat plans for Britalleebumbia."

"Rene carried this Maharaja promotion off better than anyone else I know could have," station manager Bill Hughes recalled. "He had a feeling for this kind of zany thing."

Clowning around at Joyce Dayton's with Esther; Esther's friend and co-worker, Freda; Jeannine; and Joyce Dayton, circa 1963.

CHAPTER 4
THE ATTIC

In October 1963, Rene—still looking for the next get-rich scheme—went into partnership with Machelle ("Chickie") Frankel and her husband, Nathan, to convert a warehouse into the Attic coffee house on West Broadway and Alma in Kitsilano.

Chickie's cousin Dianne Hestrin Goldberg says that Nathan Frankel did not get involved with the day-to-day operations of the Attic. "Nate dabbled in a variety of what I call business activities, always looking to make the next big deal," says Goldberg. "From what I recall, he likely put in some money to get the Attic off the ground, but my recollections are that it was a fragile financial endeavour. I think Rene was a contact Nathan had made along the way."

The Frankels had moved to Vancouver from Winnipeg a few years before. Nathan was the general manager of Tri-State Acceptance, a finance and loans company, and Chickie was a thirty-year-old musician and mother of three small children. She played the banjo, the Autoharp, folk guitar, and bongos. She had a great singing voice and wrote her own music. Chickie was active in Voice of Women, a national movement that formed in 1960 to promote peace and disarmament, and she quickly got caught up in the resurgence of folk music that was happening across North America.

By the late 1950s, the coffee house culture that was flourishing south of the border came to Vancouver. Local folk groups and solo performers shared the stages with professional Canadian and international folk artists, and people went to listen to the performers, not to dance or to talk over them. The coffee houses sprang up near the University of British Columbia campus in Point Grey and the city's downtown area and became a magnet for high school and university students and young professionals, offering them a cultural, social, and political alternative to the mainstream. The Question Mark coffee house at West Broadway and Collingwood opened in 1959 and billed itself as Western Canada's Folk Song Centre. Local entrepreneur Howie Bateman owned the Inquisition Coffee House at 726 Seymour Street, Les Stork ran the Bunkhouse Coffeehouse on Davie Street, and a network of more informal "hootenannies" existed at UBC, in private homes, and in one-time-only rented venues around the city.

Vancouver was still a city with small-town values wedged in the 1950s. Men wore suits, women wore frocks, and the Lord's Day Act prohibited business transactions on Sundays. That meant no movies, no sports events, and most certainly no booze. Nightclubs like the Commodore Ballroom or the Penthouse were not licensed, and if you wanted a hard drink you smuggled in a bottle, put it under the table, paid exorbitant prices for a mixer, and hoped that the police didn't raid the joint and confiscate your booze. If you just wanted a beer, you went to a beer parlour—women through one entrance, men though another, but never on Sundays.[8]

In 1963, Vancouver was basically divided into two different elements—a very large conservative community with a 1950s mindset, and the beatniks, a small bohemian arts community that lived mostly in low-cost West End housing. The beatniks offered some cultural resistance, drank at the Sylvia Hotel, and were mostly caught up with folk music, jazz, and poetry.

The spirit of the 1950s lived well into the '60s. In July 1962, US stand-up comic Lenny Bruce performed at Isy's Supper Club to a

8   In 1963, the Liquor Control Board authorized the removal of neon signs advertising "Men's Entrance" and "Ladies and Escorts," but many beer parlours hung on to them for another decade. Robert Campbell, "Ladies and Escorts: Gender Segregation and Public Policy in British Columbia Beer Parlours, 1925–1945," *BC Studies* 105/106 (Spring/Summer 1995): 119–38.

The Folkmasters—Pete Wyborn, Alan McRae, and Kel Winsey—with American visitor Guy Carawan on the left, performing at the Question Mark in 1960. (Courtesy Gary Cristall)

packed house. Jack Wasserman attacked his show—a blend of satire, politics, religion, and sex—and Isy Walters was told his licence would be suspended unless he cancelled the rest of Bruce's performances. Howie Bateman offered to hold the remaining performances at the Inquisition Coffee House but had to back out after the city's licensing boss descended and threatened to lift his licence.[9]

When the Attic opened in 1963, it featured performances by local artists that included the Jubilation Singers, the Wee Folks, and Claire Klein Osipov, a Jewish folksinger who sang in Yiddish. Osipov, who retired in 2016 at eighty-four, was a good friend of Chickie's, and an accomplished singer who regularly appeared on CBC radio and television. "The Attic was a wonderful little dark place and had a real coffee house atmosphere,

---

9   David Spaner, *Dreaming in the Rain: How Vancouver Became Hollywood North by Northwest* (Vancouver: Arsenal Pulp Press, 2003), 35.

where everybody smoked," says Osipov. "It was a great idea to open a coffee house because that's when folk music was at its height."

The coffee house quickly became known for the quality of its folk and blues singers, including Scottish folksinger Jean Redpath and US blues singer Barbara Dane—a student of Bessie Smith. Dane played at the Attic from November 7 to 16, 1963—for the cover price of $1.50 for adults and $1.25 for students. She had come straight from performing at the renowned Ash Grove in Los Angeles, a folk and blues club that attracted such legends as Muddy Waters, Pete Seeger, Johnny Cash, Joan Baez, Arlo Guthrie, and Kris Kristofferson.

Bob Cain was a Vancouver photographer who used to frequent the coffee houses. He remembers dropping into the Attic. "We used to go to the coffee houses quite a bit. Everybody wore ties, and they served really good coffee," he says. Cain remembers small round tables with candles. The Attic was intimate, seating about fifty people. There was a cover charge to get in, and no booze was served or allowed, says Cain. "You snapped your fingers instead of clapping," he says. "It was more of a date night. If you wanted to have a drink you'd go to a bar later or to a bottle club on Main Street."

Rene was particularly impressed with one of Chickie's compositions, a folk song named "Jewel of the West" that expressed her love for the beauty of the province. He had the Jubilation Singers record a demo, and he took it to CKNW's Hal Davis, thinking the station might be interested in using the song as its musical theme.

"I frankly didn't expect anything to come of the 'audition' and was more than merely surprised to receive a telephone call from Hal asking if I'd come in to talk with him," said Chickie.[10]

Davis took the song to the BC Association of Broadcasters with a proposal to have the association promote it as their theme song to

---

10   Machelle "Chickie" Frankel, "Jewel of the West (Beautiful BC)," *British Columbia Sheet Music*, http://bcsheetmusic.ca/htmpages/jewelofthewest.html.

By 1964, the Attic was gone, replaced by the Ark, which brought in many of the same folk acts. (Courtesy Julia and Jerry Kruz)

mark the 1967 celebration of Confederation. The association loved the idea and hired an arranger to create six different versions reflecting their different member stations' musical genres—folk, bossa nova, rock, big band, big band with vocals, and choral—and had the song professionally recorded at CBC's Vancouver studios and released on RCA Victor.

Chickie's simple folk tune became the province's official centennial theme song, marking both the 100th anniversary of the union of Vancouver Island and the mainland in 1966 and the celebration of Canadian Confederation the following year.

A little over a month after the Attic opened, on November 22, 1963, US President John F. Kennedy was assassinated. An American folk singer scheduled to perform that week was too upset to go on, and because they couldn't replace him on such short notice, the club was forced to close. On the heels of his cancellation, an America folk duo took a lucrative contract in the US, and the local groups that were brought in to replace these acts weren't well received. The ads in the *Ubyssey* stopped in late November, and the partners decided to cut their losses and close the club.

On October 2, 1964, a year after the Attic had opened, new owner Walt Robertson took an ad out in the *Ubyssey* announcing the coffee house's rebirth as the Ark. "The Attic has gone and in its place stands a new coffee house," went the ad. "The Ark is a completely remodelled version of that old barn, and the result is a warm, intimate place where one can drink coffee while Robertson, captain of the Ark, has a strict policy of top entertainment only." But like its predecessor, the Ark lasted for only a few months.

By 1964, the British Invasion had hit North America, and the coffee shops were too small and intimate for rock and pop music or for dancing. In many ways, 1964 was the turning point for Vancouver. Huge changes were happening across the border as Vietnam War protests exploded, race riots gripped large cities, and the Civil Rights Act was signed, outlawing discrimination based on race, colour, religion, sex, or national origin. Up in BC, the conservative Social Credit Party may have governed the province, but its people were restless and no longer willing to put up with the banning of novels or movies and other restrictions of earlier decades.

Although the Attic had folded, Rene's broadcasting and promotions career was just getting going. The audacious Maharaja promotion was a huge success, and Bill Hughes hired Rene in February 1964 with a monthly salary of $375 plus talent fees, which brought his salary to around $5,500 a year (equivalent to approximately $44,000 in 2018).

For the first time in his life, Rene had financial stability and a dream job that fit his personality. His new-found celebrity status soon caught the attention of the station's switchboard operator, a pretty young widow named Lolly Miller.

Lolly Miller after the inquest into the death of Esther Castellani. (Photo by Dan Scott, courtesy *Vancouver Sun*, December 1966)

CHAPTER 5

THE DIZZY DIALLER MEETS LOLLY

Rene proved to be a talented writer who could also do his own voice-overs and promotions. He started with little fifteen-second skits called *Boss and Bean* that drew in the listeners. The skit would go something like:

"Hey, boss?"

"Yeah, Bean."

"I had to take my kangaroo to the doctor."

"Why?"

"He was getting jumpy."

Former CKNW reporter George Garrett remembers Rene as "a fun guy. He was so funny on the air and off the air. He was very congenial and very smart."

As the Dizzy Dialler, Rene would phone unsuspecting people on the air and make outrageous requests. Once, he called a pet shop owner and asked if he was doing the right thing by cleaning his pet budgie with a pencil eraser. "None of it was really vindictive at all. It was all in fun," says Garrett. "It would embarrass people once they found out they were being had, but that was okay."

Another classic Dizzy Dialler was when Rene phoned the Harrison Hot Springs Hotel. He told a staff member that he had just been entertaining with trained fleas at a convention there, and one of his pet fleas had gone missing. He told her that the flea would have taken refuge in the hotel's carpet and asked her to put the phone down near the carpet while he yelled, "Here, Pooky, Pooky."

Then he would do his "You've just been had by the Dizzy Dialler" line.

Esther, Jeannine, and Rene Castellani with Karl Luond at a picnic, circa 1960.

He became so well known for this that often his unsuspecting callers would catch on quickly and say, "I know who this is—it's the Dizzy Dialler." Most people had a favourite Dizzy Dialler skit. Grohmann says his was the one when Rene phoned Olympia Tailors on East Hastings Street.

Rene: "Hello, Olympia Tailors. Do you do custom-made suits?"

Tailors: "Yes, we do."

Rene: "What kind of material?"

Tailors: "Oh, we've got all kinds of materials."

This went back and forth for another twenty-five questions or so, says Grohmann. "Then Rene told this guy on the phone that he was in town with the circus over at the PNE grounds, and he said he needed a suit in a hurry, and you could imagine the Olympia Tailor guy thinking, 'Oh, this will be good. He needs it in a hurry, and he's with the circus, so I'll probably make a lot of money.' And then Rene says, 'What time tomorrow is a good time to bring the gorilla over?' And there is this long pause and the guy at Olympia says, 'Gorilla?' And Rene finishes with the punchline—'Yes, we want a suit for the gorilla.'"

Jeannine showing off her new Christmas dress from Joyce Dayton's to her mother, circa 1963.

In December 1963, Margie and Cameron Scott and their small son, Fraser, moved into the duplex next door to the Castellanis, and the two couples immediately struck up a close friendship. "We saw them a lot and we went out with them occasionally," Margie Scott said. "Esther worked, and I used to help look after Jeannine and this kind of thing. We were very friendly with them."

Scott said that during the time that they were neighbours Esther and Rene seemed happy together. "They were always very gay people, and we thought they were both charming and we used to go out to the beach for the day with them sometimes," she said. "They were very good fun and on good terms with one another and we thought it a very happy marriage."

Jeannine remembers a happy house in those days too and says that Christmas was a big deal in the family, usually spent either with Esther's parents or at her sister Gloria's. "They had such a big house compared to ours, and we'd get to go downstairs where they had a Hawaiian rec room and we'd hula dance. I spent a lot of time with my mum," says Jeannine. "I look at pictures of us and they make me cry because I'm so happy in all of them."

Jeannine also remembers the occasional Christmas spent with another aunt, Rene's sister Rose MacIlroy, at her North Vancouver house. "My aunt played the piano beautifully. She could play by ear just like my dad," says Jeannine. "They lived up at the top of Lonsdale and the house looked out on Vancouver. The grand piano was up there, and I remember Mum and Dad dancing and playing the piano, and my Aunt Louise was there—just really fun, happy times. I had my party dress on. My mum always dressed up and my dad always looked nice, and they both loved to laugh."

The family often ate out. Jeannine remembers being with her mum and dad at the Cave and getting Wayne Newton's autograph. And they were at Iaci's all the time. "I don't even know how many times a week," says Jeannine. "We never sat in the restaurant. We were always in the kitchen where they were cooking for the people in the restaurant." Eva Iaci taught Esther to make cream puffs and cheesecake. When it got late, Jeannine and any other children who were still around were put to sleep in Eva's downstairs suite. "I found out later that, once, I was lying down on top of all the booze. When the police came in [to check for the illicit alcohol], they never checked the bed because they saw me there, sound asleep."

Frank's sisters Koko, Teenie, and Toots, says Jeannine, were straight out of some crazy sitcom—unique and quirky. "Oh man, they were funny," she says. And Frank and Rene were always doing some kind of comedy routine.

The comedy routines that Rene performed with Frank translated easily into his different radio personas at CKNW, and the Dizzy Dialler

Frank Iaci with his second wife, Marjorie, at Iaci's
restaurant, 1022 Seymour Street, 1950s.

turned Rene into a radio personality. In some ways, Rene was now
the face of CKNW. He was well liked at the station, and he caught the
attention of the nighttime receptionist, Lolly Miller.

In March 1962, twenty-two-year-old Adelaide Ann Miller started
as a switchboard operator at CKNW, working the 4:30 p.m. to midnight
shift. No one called her Adelaide, though; she'd always been known as
Lolly—after her grandmother. "We used to call her Lolly the Dolly,"
says George Garrett. "She was quite well endowed and she was an
attractive gal."

Lolly was married to Donald Miller, a twenty-six-year-old truck
driver. They had a toddler named Don and lived in a new house in the
suburb of Coquitlam. Six months after she started at the station, her
husband died in a boating accident, and she was left with a $25,000
settlement from his insurance company. Rumours quickly started

Lolly and Don Miller's wedding, April 6, 1959. (Courtesy Don Miller)

around the station that Lolly may have helped him along the way, but they weren't true.

Donald Miller had met twenty-one-year-old Elizabeth Anne May in New Westminster the week before. He told her he was upset with his wife and invited her along on a hunting trip to Harrison Hot Springs, a resort town about eighty miles (130 kilometres) from Vancouver. They arrived at midnight, after a stop to buy a case of beer, and had Miller's boat in the water by one a.m. May later told police that they had stopped to sleep on one of the small islands in Harrison Lake. The next day, Miller tried to shoot some deer without success, went back out on the lake, and continued to drink the rest of the beer and a bottle of rum.

"He sat at the back of the boat," May told police. "Then he went overboard." May thought he was fooling around and told him to get back in the boat. "I thought he was doing this to scare me so I would jump in the water after him."

When she didn't see him come up, she called for help, but it was too late. He'd drowned in twelve feet (almost four metres) of water. The police investigation confirmed that his death was an accident, noting that his blood-alcohol level of 0.23 percent "would greatly reduce his equilibrium both in the boat and in the water." There was an autopsy and an inquest, and on September 18, 1962, Lolly signed her husband's death certificate.

CKNW news reporter Barrie McMaster didn't know Lolly well but often stopped for a quick chat when they were both working the afternoon shift. "She was good to work with, intelligent, pretty—even in disposition," he says. "We had few deep conversations because she was out there at switchboard and we were in our glorified broom closet with phones, tape machines, and three teletypes churning out canary newsprint like our forest industry depended on it. She was simply a nice lady."

Lolly soon caught the attention of Bobby Hughes. Hughes had started as a writer in the copy department at CKNW in 1960. He'd gone to King Edward High School with Jack Cullen, and they were close friends. Hughes was a well-known singer in Vancouver, sang on Cullen's show, performed in the Nabob *Harmony House* musical variety show at the Orpheum Theatre, and on the CBC. And when he wasn't performing, he worked as an advertising model and copywriter.

"She was pretty, but she had a broken nose," he told Chuck Davis in *Top Dog!* "I remember when she got the insurance money after Don drowned, it was $25,000. I suggested to her she use some of the money to get her nose fixed, but she didn't."

Erm Fiorillo, station comptroller, happened to mention Hughes's interest in Lolly to Rene and was surprised by his reaction. "He became

During the 1950s and '60s, New Westminster–based CKNW, the Top Dog, was a familiar sight in the community. Wally Garrett broadcasting from a remote radio booth at the PNE in 1953. (Vancouver Archives #180-2127)

quite agitated about it, and I thought that was rather unusual for him to show this kind of interest," said Fiorillo. "A day or two later, I brought up the name again and the association with Lolly, and he told me that he had taken her under his wing and was going to talk to her in a fatherly fashion about this association. I thought this was rather unusual, so I discussed it with another staff member, and he felt as I did, that there was something between the two of them."

If Lolly and Rene thought they were being discreet, they were quite wrong. "It was common knowledge that he was having an affair with the telephone receptionist Lolly Miller," says Norm Grohmann. "We all knew that he and Lolly were an item."

Rene told Esther that his job at CKNW was keeping him much too busy to take a holiday that year. And in early August, Jeannine and Esther left for California with her parents and stayed with Mabel's sister in San Francisco for three weeks.

By this time, the rumours about Rene and Lolly's affair had reached Fiorillo, and he was finding it hard to ignore. He had hired Lolly in 1962 and was her direct supervisor. He was impressed by Rene's promotional talents, worked well with him, and, like most people at the station, liked him. But Fiorillo was upset that Rene was ruining the receptionist's reputation and his own marriage. "I thought perhaps I could do something by talking to him, so I took him out for lunch one day," said Fiorillo. "I told him that there were rumours that he and Lolly were carrying on. I wanted to bring it up to him and see if there was anything [I could do] because it could cost him his job. He told me that he was astonished, that he didn't even know where Lolly lived."

Later that month, Fiorillo was waiting for the light to change on his way to a CKNW function at the Villa Hotel when he saw Rene drive the CKNW van up Smith Avenue. "I wondered at the time why the van should be there or why he was going in this direction, and I thought it unusual, so out of curiosity, I phoned the office and asked who of our staff lived on Smith Avenue. I was informed that it was Lolly Miller," says Fiorillo. "The rumours continued to persist at the station about their association, but he was not under my jurisdiction."

Rene often took eleven-year-old Jeannine with him to the station's offices, which were then in an old building in New Westminster. He introduced Jeannine to Jack Webster, Jack Cullen, and Lolly. "He would say, 'Oh, come on, you like to play secretary, and Lolly can show you how to answer calls.' He'd say, 'She's a nice lady and she's got a little boy. He'd be like the brother that you never had.' And he got me warmed up to her that way and we became buddies," says Jeannine.

More than fifty years later, Jeannine asks: "How could a human being that is supposed to be your dad and somebody's husband do this, knowing full well what he was doing? That was evil. That was sheer evil."

Police try to hold back thousands of Beatles fans at Empire Stadium, August 22, 1964. (From the collection of Rob Frith, owner of Neptoon Records)

CHAPTER 6

THE BEATLES

By late August 1964, most of Vancouver's attention—at least if you were a teenage girl—was on the impending arrival of the Beatles and their performance at Empire Stadium. Jeannine, like many other eleven-year-olds in Vancouver, had been glued to the television when the Beatles made their historic first appearance on *The Ed Sullivan Show* on February 9, 1964. She was excited that her father had managed to get tickets for the concert and that her mother would be taking her.

In an attempt to get all listeners tuning in to CKNW for the concert that night, the promotions department hired four actors, put them in black mop-top wigs, and sent them out to drive around town in a limo. CKNW deejays invited listeners to call in if they had a "Beatles sighting," even though the real Beatles weren't expected to arrive until early that evening.

"[The Beatles] were greeted in time-honoured Vancouver tradition with a riot," wrote Tom Harrison for the *Province* in 1997. "Screaming girls, broken barricades, police motorcades, confused media, outraged public—but this city had never seen anything like it and responded accordingly."

After appearances by Bill Black's Combo, the Exciters, the Righteous Brothers, and Jackie DeShannon, the Beatles took the stage just before 9:30 p.m. and performed in front of more than 20,000 screaming fans. Jeannine was all dressed up in a wide, white pleated skirt, navy-blue blazer, and red top. She and Esther planned to meet her dad in the CKNW press booth at the stadium after the broadcast of the concert. Although Rene was part of the promotions department,

Jeannine Castellani and her cousin, Susie Luond, all dressed up in matching outfits and looking at Beatles albums at Park Royal Shopping Centre, West Vancouver, 1964.

he was often brought in as "extra station talent," says Barrie McMaster. "Hal Davis knew good talent when he heard it, and Rene was some of the sparkle on the air."

The concert opened with "Twist and Shout." Those who weren't already screaming started then and continued right through to the end of the show, drowning out hits such as "A Hard Day's Night," "All My Loving," and "I Want to Hold Your Hand." The Beatles performed eleven songs all told, finished on "Long Tall Sally," and then made a fast getaway out of the stadium. But although the concert may have been short, it's considered one of the most legendary in Vancouver's history, along with Elvis Presley's show at the same venue seven years earlier.

"The girl behind me was screaming and screaming until she vomited, and it splashed up onto my back," says Jeannine. "My mum and I spent most of the night in the washroom trying to wipe the vomit off." The washroom might have been the safest place in the stadium.

Ticket stubs from the Beatles concert at Empire Stadium. (From the collection of Rob Frith, owner of Neptoon Records)

As police inspector Bud Errington told a *Vancouver Sun* reporter, he'd never seen anything like it. "These people have lost all ability to think. Every policeman there was happy they didn't have to pack away seriously injured children. One hundred policemen were there—that's all that stood between the way it wound up and a national tragedy." What concerned police the most were the thousands of teenagers outside the stadium gates held back by only a 4-foot (1.2-metre) fence and some burly policemen.

CKNW broadcast live from the show with Jack Cullen and Rene Castellani in the press booth and Jack Webster, Jack Wasserman, and Barrie McMaster providing commentary. A taped recording of the concert survives. As the Beatles were cranking out the "yeah, yeah, yeahs" in "She Loves You," Rene told Cullen that he could see police trouble. Webster jumped in to say that a young girl had been hurt after the crowd broke down the barriers. "The police are pushing and the crowds are pushing and a girl got hurt," he said. "It's a wild night at Empire Stadium," added Cullen. "It's kind of fun watching it."

"All the lights have been put on the stadium now and you can see the kids piled up against the crash barrier. There are at least sixteen or eighteen in the first aid room now, and a number of youngsters have been arrested," reported Webster. "I can see a policeman holding this broken door to try and keep the crowds out. The crowd have been told if they don't behave themselves the concert will be cancelled."

The Beatles attend a media conference just before their Vancouver concert on August 22, 1964. (From the collection of Rob Frith, owner of Neptoon Records)

At one point on the tape, you can hear Jack Webster trying to calm down a near-hysterical Jack Wasserman. Wasserman asked, "Are you ready to run?" and Webster replied, "No, no, I think everything is under control." Wasserman said, "It's an absolute damn disgrace. I told them it's a police matter, I told them, I told them. This is the most poorly organized event in the history of Vancouver."

"Police are now using two-by-fours to hold back the stress barriers," Webster told the listeners. "They have called in reinforcements from the fire department."

Although it was hardly a riot, a frenzy of girls, many as young as eight years old, were in the throes of mass hysteria, passing out and being carried off before they were crushed by the surging crowd.

"We are back here in our broadcasting booth, and from here we can see a tremendous amount of girls being carried out," reported Rene. "The firemen are rushing out, the St. John's Ambulance—anyone who can carry these girls off the field. I don't know where they are taking them all, but in ten minutes if this goes on the whole stadium will be carried out."

Barrie McMaster says he was working a typical three to eleven p.m. news shift for CKNW when he was told to head to Empire Stadium. "I have covered a lot of things, but never in my life have I heard a sound of that many thousands of early teens completely in hysteria—shrieking. It literally hurt your ears," he says. "The girls were so excited that they would pass out, and there was a real worry that somebody was going to get crushed in front of the old PNE gates. So as these young boppers fainted and fell, we—even Jack Wasserman and Jack Webster—would pass their limp bodies over the fence to somebody else who would take them to first aid."

Over the lyrics to "If I Fell," Cullen admitted to Rene that he just didn't get it. "I'm part of the Sinatra era," he said.

Then Cullen noticed a black limousine pulling up alongside the stage. "I bet you that when the Beatles come off stage, they're not going to any dressing room. They'll be whisked out of here and in that limousine, out of this stadium, right back to the airport, and out of town as quick as they can. And I think it's a good idea," he said.

As the Beatles launched into "Long Tall Sally," another limousine pulled up, along with fifteen police motorcycles. "They are leaving now," said Cullen. "They are not walking off, they are running off, they are running to the cars. They are behind the stage, and I believe that they are getting in the cars. Boy, that's what I call quick."

"The Beatles could have been bank robbers the way they trucked out of there," added Webster. "They are still carrying bodies out, but they are not anticipating any more trouble. Maybe it's just beginning to break through to the crowd now that the Beatles have gone."

"We've always said that our police department was a good police department, and they proved it tonight, Jack," said Rene.

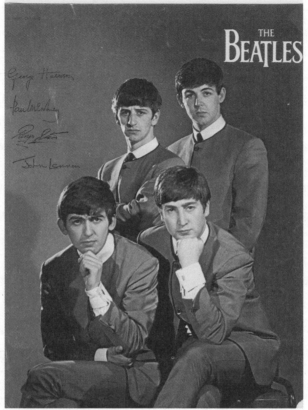

Autographed photo. (From the collection of Rob Frith, owner of
Neptoon Records)

Even with the pandemonium, Cullen managed to get in a few
plugs for sponsor Kits Cameras. The wily Cullen had taped CKNW's
broadcast off a direct feed from the public address system. Several years
later, he released it as a bootleg album of the concert. He managed to
press a thousand copies before Capitol Records found out and made
him stop. The recording quickly became a collector's item.

UBC psychologist Dr J.E. Ryan attended the concert and wrote
a column for the *Province*. Dr Ryan noted that the audience was in
a state "of almost complete loss of emotional control," and many
exhibited a tremendous amount of anxiety. "In our society, children

are taught to repress it. They build up steam like a boiler and there has to be a form of release. A release of tensions is generally good—but there must be better ways than The Beatles provide," wrote Dr Ryan. "However, it is better they go wild over The Beatles than become juvenile delinquents or become mentally ill." With full disclosure, Dr Ryan acknowledged that he hated their music and was relieved that it was "just a fad."

Dr Ryan was wrong, of course. The concert itself was less of a music event and more of a cultural phenomenon. "In less than half an hour, the Beatles had changed the course of rock 'n' roll in Vancouver," wrote *Province* music critic Tom Harrison. "Vancouver was never the same after the Beatles."

Jeannine wasn't too disappointed to miss most of the twenty-seven-minute concert. Her dad managed to get Paul McCartney's autograph and swipe a packet of Ringo Starr's cigarettes.

In the weeks that followed the concert, Esther continued to put up a brave front for Jeannine, but as she confided in her close friend Margie Scott, she had discovered a letter to Rene from someone called Lolly, and she was receiving disturbing anonymous phone calls from a woman late at night.

Mabel Luond with Esther and Jeannine Castellani on Granville Street, circa 1960.

CHAPTER 7
LOVE, LOLLY

Margie Scott and her husband moved to North Vancouver, where they opened a veterinary practice in October 1964, but she and Esther stayed friends and kept in close contact. About a month after her move, Scott and her mother dropped by to visit Esther.

"While we were there, Esther confided in us that Rene came in late one night, fell asleep on the chesterfield, and she went through his wallet and found a letter," said Scott. "She told us the contents of the letter. As far as I remember, it was a letter written from Hawaii from Lolly to Rene that said, 'It was lovely to hear your voice. Love, Lolly.'"

Esther told them that she had confronted Rene with this letter, and he admitted he had been seeing this woman but told her that they were not sleeping together, that he only went to see her to talk and drink coffee. "She was so unhappy about this. Later she got a phone bill for sixty dollars. Rene told her he'd phoned Lolly in Hawaii," said Scott.

As always, Rene had an explanation. He told Esther that Lolly was the receptionist at CKNW who had been helping out on a promotion where listeners joined deejay Gerry Davies on a tour of the Hawaiian Islands. Rene said that he had a potential buyer for some of his Dizzy Dialler tapes who lived in Hawaii, and Rene was phoning Davies to see if he could find his address. Davies was out, and Lolly happened to answer the phone. "It's what she does," he told her.

Scott and her mother visited Esther again about a week before Christmas to give Jeannine a present. "Nothing was said until Jeannine went to bed. Esther told us that she had been keeping tabs on Rene, as he was staying out late at night and sometimes went out at three in the morning, saying he had to make his tapes for the following day," said Scott.

Shortly after Esther confronted Rene about the letter from Lolly and his subsequent phone call to Hawaii, she started feeling ill.

The first time she felt sick to her stomach was after attending the Hadassah Bazaar with her mother in October 1964, but she put it down to overeating. But her nausea continued, and she told her friend and co-worker Palmira McKillap that she was getting a burning sensation in her stomach. She decided to cut back on coffee, and the burning sensation cleared up soon after that. "It was just infrequent after that, nothing specific," said McKillap.

Just before Christmas, Esther had gone to a party at Joyce Dayton's, and the next day she was violently ill. When she came back to work, she found that when she put her hands on either side of the doorjamb and stretched, it eased the pain in her stomach. She would also frequently shake her hands and told McKillap, "These stupid hands, they always go numb."

It was probably just stomach flu, she told her boss and co-workers. She didn't need time off; she'd soldier through. She didn't tell them she couldn't stop work. Even with Rene's steady income from CKNW, they still needed the money. So she would feel sick, throw up, and then feel better.

Esther was a two-pack-a-day smoker and drank a lot of coffee. She was always trying to lose weight and usually going on or off a diet. She'd have cottage cheese on toast or nothing at all one day and eat a large meal of fried foods the next. She'd take diet pills for a few days and then stop. "We blamed her troubles on instant coffee, her poor eating habits, and dieting," said McKillap.

The family often ate out, and Esther liked to order hamburgers and fries. She loved vanilla milkshakes, especially the ones from

Esther, Rene, and Jeannine Castellani with Cocoa, circa 1964.

White Spot and the Aristocratic. Veal chops were another favourite, and she would often cook those at home. Rene liked to barbecue.

On New Year's Eve 1964, Esther and Rene went to a party at the McKillaps'. The next day she had a terrible stomach ache. She blamed it on the gin.

Early in January, she made an appointment with Dr John Sector, who had an office across the road from Esther's work. "She admitted to a number of gastronomic misadventures during this period," he wrote in his report. "She said she was very gassy and distended and that her abdominal pain radiated through to her back. Exams revealed some low-grade tenderness in the left upper quadrant. There was rather more intense tenderness in the lower left chest wall. The patient, however, was in no distress."

Sector diagnosed gastritis, cautioned Esther about her diet, and prescribed an anti-spasmodic, antacid, and a three-day course of an anti-inflammatory drug called Tandearil[11] to help with her muscular pain.

It didn't seem to help. Joyce Dayton worried that Esther couldn't keep down her food and seemed to live on tea and the odd apple. "She never went out for lunch. She was very erratic in her eating," said Dayton. "She was frightened to drink too much coffee. She thought perhaps that this is what disturbed her."[12]

Dayton said that one morning Esther told her that she had nearly fainted on her way to work. But Esther insisted on staying at work and felt better as the day went on. "She functioned very well even when she was ill or days she was complaining," said McKillap.

At the end of January 1965, Dayton was away for about eight days while the store was being painted. Esther and McKillap helped out by painting some of the trim so that the store could reopen quickly. Esther had told McKillap that she was getting anonymous phone calls late at night, when Rene was supposedly at work, from a woman asking her if she knew he was going around with someone named Lolly. When Esther confronted Rene, he told her that it was just someone being malicious. But Esther didn't believe him and was very upset.

In February, Esther's health seemed to improve. She had not seen Dr Sector since her visit in early January and was now working full time at Joyce Dayton's boutique. But although her health was stable,

11   Tandearil was an anti-inflammatory drug taken off the market in the mid-1980s because of a link to bone marrow suppression and Stevens–Johnson syndrome, which starts with flu-like symptoms followed by a painful rash that spreads and blisters.

12   Esther wasn't alone in her love and fear of coffee. In 1963, David Suzuki, a rising star in the UBC genetics department, cited research that showed three or four cups of coffee did "150 times as much chromosome damage as one day of fallout during periods of nuclear testing." Quoted in Lawrence Aronsen, *City of Love and Revolution: Vancouver in the Sixties* (Vancouver: New Star Books, 2010) 88.

she knew that her marriage was not. As Frank Iaci later testified at the inquest, he had lived in Las Vegas for about a year and was getting ready to move back to Vancouver when he received a phone call from Esther. "Esther called me one night to tell me that the marriage had gone bad and Rene had found somebody else and could I please rush home and help her. What she had hoped for me to do, I don't know," he said.

Rumours about Rene and Lolly's affair continued to fly around CKNW and eventually reached Bill Hughes, the station manager. Although Rene had no set hours and often stayed late into the evenings to work on promotions, he was often absent when Esther called looking for him. Hughes had received complaints from the morning switchboard operators, who were uncomfortable about Esther calling the station looking for her husband. One operator said that Esther had phoned asking for him at 8:45 one morning, and when she told Esther that he had not arrived at the station, Esther had said, "That's funny. He said he had some very important program bulletins that he had to have out ready for the morning, and he had left home around 4:00 a.m." The afternoon operator had also complained. After she had told Esther that Rene had left for the afternoon, Rene took her to task the next day for giving out information about his whereabouts.

"At first I discounted the rumours and didn't say anything. I just said that these were rumours, and if this is all people talk about they should be busier," said Hughes. "But the rumours persisted." Hughes said he was unable to ignore the gossip when he learned that the CKNW truck that Rene drove had been seen parked outside Lolly's home at three in the morning.

"I felt it was my responsibility to bring Rene into my office and ask him if there was any truth to the rumours and just what was going on. I told him that while what he did in his off time was his own business, that I would not tolerate it when there was a station vehicle or station time involved." Rene told Hughes that there was nothing to the rumours. Lolly had phoned him at the station when he was working late one night and told him that her son was sick and she needed a prescription filled.

"I asked what time that would be, and he said it was around 12:30 or one in the morning. All I observed was that I did not know of any drugstores in that area which were open for prescription filling at that time of the night." Hughes told Rene that if there was something going on, he should stop it immediately, or both he and Lolly would be fired.

Meanwhile, Erm Fiorillo, Lolly's direct boss, was becoming increasingly concerned about the rumours of a workplace affair. Fiorillo had trained as a teacher, then served in the air force during the war. After his discharge, he became the business manager for a small fishing and towing business and learned accounting. He had worked at CKNW since 1950. He was much more than the station's accountant, though; he was a thoughtful and compassionate man, a devout Roman Catholic, and he was disturbed by the affair from a moral standpoint. Fiorillo was concerned about how it would reflect on the station. He also hated being lied to.

Fiorillo called Lolly into his office and told her that he had had a number of complaints about her work on the switchboard. "After chewing her out about the complaints and warning her that one more complaint would bring dismissal, I brought up the rumour that she and Rene were interested in one another, and she denied it. I said that I didn't understand why she would deny it when Rene had admitted to Bill Hughes that his car was parked outside her apartment at a very early hour one morning. This statement really stunned Lolly, and she didn't say anything, so I asked her to show a little common sense—since Rene didn't appear to be showing any—before he damaged both his reputation and hers. I also told Lolly that what she did outside of the station was her own business, but what went on inside the station was my business, and if I had any more complaints about her that she'd be out of a job. I did not again discuss the matter with Lolly, despite the persistence of rumours that the two were carrying on an affair."

In February 1965, Lolly moved from her apartment to a basement suite in a house owned by her former neighbours Ronald and Sylvia Smail. Rene helped her move into the suite and became a frequent visitor. The couple would pop upstairs to visit with the Smails. "Often on these occasions the discussion was on Lolly and Rene getting married as soon as Rene got his divorce," said Smail. "One evening, Rene came upstairs and visited with me. I asked him how his divorce was going. As I recall, he said it was completed."

It's likely that Rene was lying not only to the Smails but to Lolly about his divorce. And by all accounts, he never discussed divorce with Esther.

Prior to 1968, when Parliament passed the first federal Divorce Act, divorce in British Columbia fell under the antiquated UK Matrimonial Causes Act of 1857. According to Roderick Phillips of Carleton University and author of *Untying the Knot: A Short History of Divorce*, that meant the only grounds for divorce were for adultery, and divorce was by mutual consent—or not at all. Even this came with a double standard. Although a husband could obtain a divorce if his wife cheated, a wife had to prove that her husband was not only cheating but also engaging in desertion, bigamy, rape, sodomy, incestuous adultery, or bestiality.[13] If you wanted a divorce because

---

13 Kristen Douglas, "Divorce Law in Canada," paper 96-3E, Law and Government Division, March 27, 2001, http://publications.gc.ca/Collection-R /LoPBdP/CIR/963-e.htm.

you'd met someone else or fallen out of love, you had to endure five years of separation first.

If this wasn't bad enough, there was quite a bit of public shaming that went along with the process. You had to publicize your intent to divorce in the *Canada Gazette* and in the *Vancouver Sun* or another daily for six months. The notice would include the date and place of marriage and details of the marital breakdown, as well as the name of the person the spouse was having an affair with.[14]

"Historically, murder was one of the ways of getting out of a marriage, as were desertion and bigamy," says Phillips. "If Esther hadn't committed adultery, wasn't agreeable to a collusive divorce—by admitting, falsely, that she had been adulterous—and wasn't prepared to divorce Rene for adultery, then there were no options for a legal termination of the marriage," he says. "Rene could have simply deserted Esther and lived with the other woman, of course. They could have left BC and lived elsewhere as man and wife and maybe got away with it—as many people did in the days before centralized and computerized records, social media, and so on. But Rene seems to have been weirdly fastidious, perhaps wanting to 'do the right thing' for the other woman."

As a man consumed with his image and his position in the community, and to a lesser extent the Roman Catholic Church, divorce would have been a disgraceful admission of defeat. "His image was really important to him, and he wanted to upgrade it," says forensic psychologist Dr Heather Burke. "He didn't just want to leave Esther and go off with Lolly. He wanted it all above board so he would look good. And that's probably one of the reasons that he liked Lolly—because his wife was older and overweight, and he wanted to portray a more

---

14   Acts of Divorce, 1841–1968, Library and Archives Canada.

youthful image. Lolly fit that image. She was young, beautiful, and had money."

But getting rid of Esther wasn't going to be all that easy—it would take careful planning and ingenuity. As Esther became sicker, Rene would play the most important role of his life—that of a concerned and attentive husband, continuing to deny his love affair while murdering his wife as quickly and efficiently as possible.

Rene and Esther Castellani, circa 1964.

CHAPTER 8
TURN FOR THE WORSE

One Sunday morning in March, Esther was excited to go to a gin breakfast held by Edna Berteau at the Penthouse restaurant on top of the twenty-two-storey Georgian Towers Hotel.[15]

Edna Berteau ran the World-Wide Travel Agency, a client of CKNW. About fifty people were invited, and Esther and Rene sat with Jack Cullen and his wife. Guests were served a punch made of gin and orange juice and ate a breakfast of sausages, bacon, and eggs. The meal was catered by the legendary Frank Baker, who ran the hotel's restaurant.

"Rene and Esther were very good company, and there was lots of laughter. She was a jolly person," said Berteau. "I don't know of any incident where Rene and Esther didn't get along."

Looking back at that time, Jeannine agrees. "I never sensed any trouble as a child. I just felt that my dad wasn't home a lot, but there was never any fighting in front of me, so they were pretty good at hiding their feelings."

After the breakfast, Esther became ill with pain that radiated from her upper abdomen up to her right shoulder blade. Her back hurt, and she felt a tightness in her chest that she hadn't had before. She spent the next twelve hours nauseated and vomiting.

Rene phoned Dr John Sector, who made a house call the following night. He found Esther sitting on the chesterfield watching television. "She appeared placid, not nauseated, had a soft abdomen, normal pulse, blood pressure, temperature, and respiration," he wrote. Sector found Esther to be a bright, intelligent woman, and he also found her

---

15   The hotel building at 1450 West Georgia was converted into apartments in 1976.

a bit plump. Dr Sector figured that she had come down with a stomach ache from overeating and complained so much that her overindulgent husband had got him out of bed to attend to her. Sector told Esther that she was probably suffering from inflammation of the gallbladder, and he prescribed more medication.

Meanwhile, Sheila Luond was becoming increasingly worried about her sister-in-law. "Normally she was a very exuberant person, and she was less so. She seemed tired and not herself," she said. When Esther, Rene, and Jeannine came to the Luonds' West End apartment a few days after the visit from Dr Sector, Esther told Sheila that she still had stomach pain and might even have an ulcer. To Sheila's surprise, Esther refused a cup of coffee and drank a glass of milk instead. "I had known that she was not well prior to this, but she always made light of anything that was wrong with her," Sheila said. "That was the first time I realized that she was really sick."

Esther felt better after a few days, and she and Rene signed a lease on a larger duplex in Kerrisdale. She was happy about the upcoming move.

But she was soon back in Dr Sector's office. "The patient came to my office March 20. She said she was greatly improved," he recorded in his notes. An office visit a week later indicated further improvement. She was urged to watch her diet very carefully and start a program of weight reduction.

Then, on March 28, the family went to Iaci's restaurant for dinner, and when Esther came home she was violently ill.

The next day was her birthday. Sheila and Karl dropped in and found Esther packing and getting ready to move to the new house on West 41st. She told Sheila that she still wasn't feeling well and said her fingers were numb and "sort of felt dead." Still, Esther and Rene seemed to be getting along well, Sheila thought.

Jeannine is in the second row, third from the left, in this class photo from Little Flower Academy, circa 1962.

Esther's mother, Mabel, visited a few days after they had moved. She was surprised at the sparseness of the furnishings. "There was a living room, a dining room, kitchen, three bedrooms, and a basement," she said. "They had a chesterfield in the front room and a dining-room suite, but they didn't have a stove or anything in the kitchen, just a fridge and a hot plate to cook on. Then upstairs, there was one bedroom that had a studio bed, and that's where Esther slept with Jeannine."

Jeannine was eleven when they moved into the duplex—it would be her seventh move. "It was like we didn't fully live there. Nothing was really unpacked," says Jeannine. "Upstairs, I had my room, my bed, and all my toys, but their room wasn't put together. Their clothes were in the closet, but it was stark, the mattress was on the floor, and like the headboard wasn't attached to the bed." In retrospect, Jeannine says she found her parents' bedroom "very cold and creepy. We were alone a lot in that house. My dad was never there. I just remember Mum not feeling well, and I'd never before seen her sick. She hid it very well. Maybe she didn't want to scare me."

Esther had already confided in her friend Margie Scott that things weren't going well in the marriage. But when Scott and her mother dropped in to see Esther and she gave them a tour of her new home, they were surprised to see that although Jeannine's bedroom was properly set up, there was no double bed set up in the main bedroom. Esther told them that even in the other duplex, Rene had slept on the chesterfield.

Scott and her mother were still there when Rene arrived home around eleven that night. "Rene was glum, and they didn't speak to each other. It was quite a bad atmosphere," said Scott. "We were drinking coffee, but Esther didn't make coffee for him, and he didn't ask Esther for coffee. I noticed Rene was not his usual gay, charming self, and the conversation was directed away from each other and just to us." They left shortly afterward.

Scott said she saw Esther again toward the end of April, when Esther, Rene, and Jeannine brought Rene's sister's dog to be treated at the Scotts' veterinary clinic. Esther told her that she suspected that Rene was still seeing someone else and the marriage was shaky. Esther wanted to take a family trip to California during his two-week vacation in July, and she thought that Rene owed her that much because he hadn't taken a holiday the previous year.

Meanwhile, Sheila Luond was baffled that Esther's doctor didn't seem to know if she had an ulcer or gallbladder disease, and Esther didn't seem too interested in finding out. By mid-April, Esther was still complaining of stomach pain and generally not feeling well. "Esther seemed to get rapidly worse," said Sheila. "She was very sick and nauseous all the time and not like herself at all. She didn't look well, and while she tried to carry it off, it was obvious she was not well."

Sheila said she didn't see much of Esther during this time, but Sheila's mother-in-law was in daily contact with her. "I didn't call too frequently because her husband very often was not at home in the evening and I hesitated to phone, knowing Esther wasn't feeling very well," said Sheila. "I didn't want to disturb her."

Joyce Dayton was also worried about Esther. Esther wasn't just her assistant manager, she was also her friend. They often got together socially—at least they had until this spring when Esther became ill. Esther phoned Dayton one morning saying she couldn't come to work. She had been very sick during the night, so sick she felt that she didn't have the strength to get off the bathroom floor. When Dayton came to the house, Esther was lying on the living room sofa in her pyjamas. Dayton and Esther's other co-workers urged her to see another doctor.

Esther was off work for the first week of May but continued to feel awful. On May 6, she ate a hamburger with mushrooms and later drank a glass of milk. She felt nauseated almost immediately and seemed to deteriorate from then on.

When she hadn't returned to work after a few days, Palmira McKillap dropped around to check on her and get the key to the store. She found Esther lying on the chesterfield looking very sick. "She was complaining of terrible stomach cramps and this numbness in her hands," said McKillap.

"I remember Mother's Day that year, because I could tell that she wasn't feeling well," said Jeannine. "My dad went out and bought an old charcoal barbecue and said we're going to make hamburgers for Mother's Day. I remember thinking she's just not feeling good, but she's not going to ever say anything." That night, Esther was so ill from stomach pain and vomiting that Rene had Dr Sector make another house call. The doctor gave her an injection of Gravol and Demerol and increased her other medications.

When Esther saw Dr Sector the next day in his office, she told him she was feeling much better, apart from constipation. Two days later, he was called back for another house call. He found Esther sitting up

Between 1961 and 1965, the Castellanis lived at four different addresses, all within a few blocks of where this 1960s photo was taken at West 41st Avenue and Yew Street. (Vancouver Archives #780-136)

watching television. He gave her some Gravol for the nausea and a strict talking-to about her dietary indiscretions and asked her to come see him in his office in the next day or two.

On May 18, Esther, Rene, and Jeannine drove Cocoa the poodle over to the Scotts' North Vancouver veterinary clinic to be clipped. Margie Scott noticed that Esther's face was bloated and the tops of her arms were blue from the injections. Esther told her friend that she had been vomiting on and off for the last two weeks and couldn't work. She thought it was something that she'd eaten. She'd stopped drinking coffee altogether and had tea and a slice of watermelon. But Scott noted that she was still "jolly" Esther, who joked to her friend, "No more gin breakfasts for me!"

"I asked if she had an ulcer, and she said the doctor said her stomach was too inflamed [for that to be determined, and] he would have to wait for X-rays," said Scott.

Rene had gone out to play pool with Cameron Scott. They came back around eleven p.m., and the Castellanis left.

Dr Sector was called back to the house on May 21. Esther's nausea and vomiting had gotten worse. He told Rene that he thought it might be sodium retention, and he arranged for an X-ray to check for gallbladder disease. It was the ninth and final time Sector would treat her.

The following day—a Saturday—Esther tried to go back to work. "She came and she felt ill and weak and dizzy," said her co-worker. "We had her lie down on a big chair. She had to go home before lunch. Jeannine went home with her. I was told that she was sick to her stomach when she got home." Esther's family and co-workers had had enough. They couldn't understand why Dr Sector hadn't sent Esther for tests to figure out what was causing her symptoms.

"Esther's mother was very unhappy with her condition," said Sheila. "She told me that Rene had told her that Esther had sodium retention. I said to my mother-in-law, 'Every time I hear about her illness, it is a different sickness and no tests have been made.' We had heard of ulcers and gallbladder and sodium retention, but no tests." When she asked Rene why there had been no tests he said, "And what university did you get your degree from, Sheila?"

Mabel called Rene and told him she wanted to get a second opinion. He was furious. He resented his in-laws interfering with his wife's treatment, and he called Joyce Dayton that night and told her so. "He said to me, did they think he was not capable of caring for his own wife?"

Finally, after several phone calls from Esther's mother, he told Mabel, "For God's sake, somebody help me." Mabel replied, "Okay, Rene. You have finally said it. Now I will help. I'm calling in another doctor."

Mabel called Dr Bernard Moscovitch, a specialist in internal medicine, and asked if he would see Esther. He told her that he couldn't until Dr Sector had signed off. Rene called Dr Sector, who withdrew from the case, and Dr Moscovitch came to see Esther that night.

"Dr Sector pretty well covered the history of the previous two or three months. It was characterized by recurring bouts of abdominal pain, nausea, vomiting, and just feeling generally unwell," said Dr Moscovitch. "I examined her and found nothing to indicate active disease. I suggested to her that since she had had this series of complaints for such a long period of time, that it might be wise to consider hospitalization for complete investigation. I told her to think about this and to let me know."

The following day, a Sunday, Rene left home early, saying he had to prepare a CKNW truck for the North Vancouver May Day parade. "We were home alone, and she had been vomiting and having a hard time getting down the stairs," said Jeannine. "I can remember being frightened, thinking she was going to fall. And she called her parents, and my grandpa came and got us."

Rene arrived home about eight p.m., and Esther started to throw up an hour later. He phoned Dr Moscovitch who told them to take Esther straight to Vancouver General Hospital. Dr Moscovitch admitted Esther with a tentative diagnosis of acute gastroenteritis and suspected gallbladder disease. He took a complete medical history and found that she had felt weak and tired, and had experienced intermittent episodes of nausea, vomiting, and abdominal pain and diarrhea since the beginning of the year. "She had vague abdominal pain, but there was nothing localized in her abdomen to pinpoint an area of difficulty. Her pulse was rapid. Her blood pressure was on the low side," he said. Esther told him that she had experienced numbness and tingling in her fingers and toes for about a week or ten days prior to admission.

"I was impressed by her attitude despite the discomfort she was enduring. Mrs Castellani was a very congenial, happy-go-lucky type," he later testified at the appeal trial.

Dr Moscovitch ordered X-rays for her chest, gallbladder, and neck. When an electrocardiogram showed an abnormal disorder in the heart, he added potential heart failure to his list of concerns. Initial tests indicated that Esther was suffering from an abnormally low white blood cell count, a condition called leukopenia, and there was a breakdown of her red blood cells. These findings suggested a toxic blood condition. The next step was to try to find the source, whether it was viral or exposure to toxic substances through lead or paint.

"She looked miserable and complained of nausea and vomiting," said head nurse Lydia Ratzlaff. Because of the numbness in her hands, Esther was unable to feed herself and had to be helped with her meals. "All her food had to be cut up, and her liquids had to be poured out for her," said the nurse.

After she had been in the hospital for a few days, her mother was thrilled to find that she was improving. "She was on a sugar-free diet and getting vitamin B_{12} shots," said Mabel. "She was enjoying her food and in very good spirits." Her blood work showed improvement over the first week, and she had stopped throwing up. But the numbness and tingling were getting worse.

Rene took Jeannine to stay with his sister Louise and their mother so that she would be close to her school. He dropped Cocoa off with Margie Scott, who'd agreed to keep Jeannine's dog until the doctors found out what was wrong with Esther.

When Jeannine first went to visit her mother in the hospital, she was shocked. Esther could barely get out of bed, and when she did, she had a hard time walking. "We were trying to get her up and walk her in the hallway, and she said she couldn't feel her hands or feet. I can remember looking at her hands and thinking, why can't she feel them? She kept rubbing her fingers," said Jeannine. "And then she put her slippers on. They were those elastic type—kind of glittery, I remember.

I have those same slippers still. Grandma [Mabel Luond] kept them, and they've started to turn into powder. You hang on to things, but it's just stuff. At the end of the day, all you have left is memories."

After Esther had been in the hospital for about ten days, her sister, Gloria, came by to visit and found Esther sitting up in bed but complaining of the lack of feeling in her hands and feet. "She got up and walked but couldn't feel her feet and had to watch to put her feet down," said Gloria. "When she smoked, she had to hold her cigarette and the base of her fingers. She had to stop smoking, as she couldn't feel the cigarettes or handle them."

Gloria started to visit every day. She even brought in an orange squeezer so that Esther could drink fresh juice. "I used to rub her hands and arms and feet to help the feeling, as they were painful," said Gloria. "I went every day, and if she was sleeping, I'd go back in the evening and talk to her. I told her if she would eat, I'd get her up in a wheelchair and get her home soon."

Josephine Penner, one of Esther's nurses, said they were doing everything they could to get Esther to eat. "We would get a relative, if one was visiting, to help feed her," she said, saying it wasn't unusual to find Rene giving his wife fluids. "He appeared to be very fond of his wife and visited frequently," said Penner. "He told me that he wanted to spend as much time as possible with her. I can recall telling him he should get some sleep, as he appeared haggard. He said he didn't want to sleep, as he wanted to stay with her every minute."

Audrey Hill, a twenty-year-old nurse's aide, got to know Esther well. She would often help the nurse lift Esther from the stretcher to the bed when she could no longer get up and walk around. Hill would help Esther hold a glass so that she could drink and a spoon so that she could eat. "I'd help her turn over, and I used to roll her bed up and make sure she was comfortable," said Hill. "She had a very tiny rash all over her body that was very, very itchy. She seemed to be uncomfortable all the time."

As Esther's health worsened, Rene's colleagues were shocked that he intended to go through with the station's latest promotion, the "Guy in the Sky," because he'd be unable to visit his hospitalized wife for the nine days that he would be perched on top of Vancouver's landmark BowMac sign. "She isn't that sick," he told them.

The BowMac Sign at 1154 West Broadway, 1995. (Courtesy Patrick Gunn)

CHAPTER 9
GUY IN THE SKY

"I begged him to scrap the promotion," CKNW's sales manager Mel Cooper told the *Vancouver Sun*'s Denny Boyd in 1982. "[I told him] to spend his time with Esther. Rene said we had an obligation to the sponsor and that the show had to go on. I thought it was terribly callous, but most promo guys were a bit crazy."

Rene's personal life was spinning out of control. Neither he nor Lolly had been able to contain the rumours of their affair at CKNW, and Bill Hughes had had enough. He told their immediate supervisors to fire them both. Lolly was allowed to resign, but Rene used his wife's worsening health as an excuse and talked his way back into his job. Hughes agreed it would be unkind to drop him. As soon as Esther recovered, Hughes said, let him go.

With his wife still in hospital with an unknown disease, Rene's colleagues in the promotions department were puzzled that he still intended to go ahead with the "Guy in the Sky" promotion for the Bowell McLean Motor Company (BowMac) on West Broadway.

Rene was, as always, short of money, and the promotion paid a bonus over his regular salary. It had already been extensively advertised on CKNW, and billboards had been placed around the car lot. BowMac hired a Pinkerton guard to stay near the bottom of the sign, not only to keep people from trying to climb up the scaffolding but also to make sure that Rene kept his contractual promise not to come down. "In presenting the promotional idea to him from the client, he was told and agreed that it was nine days, twenty-four hours a day, and he could not come down," said Hughes. "I asked him to make a commitment because I did realize that his wife was ill, and he said, 'No, this is fine. She is not that ill, and I am going up.'"

The BowMac car dealership had a history of staging stunts to lure customers away from the Dueck Chevrolet Oldsmobile dealership down the road. Under Jimmy Pattison's management, promotions included dressing up a performing monkey in overalls and hiring the Leavy brothers—seven-foot-tall twins—to hang out in the used car lot. In 1958, Pattison staged the "world's largest checker game" where models in red or black bathing suits became the checkers moving across a board of two-foot squares. Pattison topped even that the following year when he commissioned Neon Products—a company that he later bought—to build a sixty-five-foot (twenty-metre) sign with orange and red letters that spelled BOWMAC and a transformer powerful enough to illuminate a city block. It was briefly North America's largest free-standing sign.[16]

And on June 4, 1965, ten days after his wife entered the hospital, Rene Castellani climbed to the top of the BowMac sign. The idea was that he would live in a station wagon that was perched on top of steel scaffolding beside the sign. He vowed not to come down until every last car in the lot was sold. The station wagon was equipped with a telephone and a direct line to the station, bedding, and a chemical toilet. Food was sent up to him in a bucket. The car was brightly lit up, and Rene was quite visible from the ground most of the time. He would give regular broadcasts from the tower. Passersby were encouraged to drive by and honk their horns, and they could see a clothesline

---

16　The BowMac sign cost $100,000, weighed twelve tons, took eight months to design and build, and employed 120 people in its structure. Each slab letter, spelling BOWMAC vertically, was ten feet (three metres) tall and just over four feet (one metre) wide. Jimmy Pattison, *Jimmy: An Autobiography* (Toronto: Seal Books, 1987), 47.

strung from the station wagon to the sign, with a pair of Rene's shorts swaying on the line.

As with most of the station promotions and special events, the announcers worked closely with the promotions department. Wally Garrett, a seventeen-year veteran with the station, broadcast from the mobile studio that was installed in a large glass-fronted trailer on the BowMac car lot. He could communicate with Rene over an intercom or just climb up the tower to sit and chat.

Erm Fiorillo had been recovering from a heart attack and hadn't seen Rene since the previous April. Shortly after he was released from hospital, he and his wife dropped by to see Rene at BowMac. Fiorillo asked how Esther was doing, and to his astonishment, Rene told him, "We almost lost Esther last week."

"I was stunned by the news, because this was the first time my wife and I were aware that Esther was seriously ill. I must honestly admit that I didn't believe him at first because of the many lies he had told me in the past," said Fiorillo. "I asked him at the time if he saw her every night, and he said that he didn't come down from the tower at all. So I didn't really think that she could be as sick as that if he didn't come down."

Rene phoned Fiorillo from the tower later that week, waking him up some time after midnight. Fiorillo asked about Esther and whether the doctors had found what was causing her illness. "He said he thought it was lead poisoning," said Fiorillo. "That she had been spraying some Christmas baubles at the place where she worked and it could have been that."

At nights, Rene worked mostly with deejay Gerry Davies. The two had known each other since 1944, when they worked in local theatre. Davies would phone Rene at 12:15, 2:15, and 4:15 in the morning to do a cut-in, and sometimes he'd call randomly "to check in with the

When the BowMac sign was completed in 1959, for a time it was North America's tallest free-standing sign. (Vancouver Archives #2008-022.071)

Guy in the Sky." Davies says that Rene was always available, except for a couple of times when he told Davies he would skip one call to get more sleep, and another time, when he told him that he wanted to go to the hospital to see Esther.

News editor Mauri Hesketh talked to Rene when he phoned the station one day. He asked him "off the record" if he really stayed up there all night. "He said something to the effect of, 'No, I can come down around three in the morning if there is no one around.'" No one ever saw him come down. Not the security guard at the car lot, not his Kerrisdale neighbours, and not one of the nurses at VGH.

While he was up there, his sister-in-law, Gloria, dropped by with a milkshake and a hamburger from Dairy Queen. She talked to him through the intercom, and he leaned out of the car window to talk to her, she said. And, even though he was not yet six, Lolly's son, Don, also remembers dropping by the BowMac lot with his mother to visit Rene and talking to him through the intercom in the broadcasting trailer at the bottom of the sign.

At three p.m. on Saturday, June 12, the entire promotions department gathered at the bottom of the sign for Rene's coming-down ceremony, which was broadcast live on CKNW. Rene's immediate boss, Glen Garvin, advertising and promotions manager, gave him the next two days off. Rene told him he was going to take the station's truck to pick up Jeannine and go visit his wife in hospital.

4987 HOY STREET . . . mentioned at inquest

—George Diack Photo

Arsenic Inquest Jury Told
Husband Planned Marriage

4987 Hoy Street. (*Vancouver Sun*, December 2, 1965)

CHAPTER 10

RENE AND LOLLY LOOK FOR A HOUSE

When Rene and Jeannine got to the hospital late Saturday afternoon, Mabel and Karl Luond were there visiting Esther. Mabel thought that during the nine days that Rene had been on top of the BowMac sign, the puffiness had left Esther's face and she looked better.

It was soon clear that Rene was not planning to stay at the hospital for long; he wanted to take Jeannine back to his sister's. Jeannine, naturally, wanted to stay with her mother. Rene kept looking at his watch, and he told his father-in-law that he had to go to a meeting for CKNW at the Bayshore hotel. "He was upsetting Jeannine, and I knew for sure there was something wrong," said Karl. Mabel took Rene out into the hall and told him to stop arguing with his daughter, that they would take Jeannine with them when they left.

Karl suspected that Rene was having an affair because Esther had told him that Rene worked at all hours throughout the day and night. "I know that a big company like CKNW would never work him from three in the morning to ten at night," Karl said. He decided to check up on Rene and see if he was really where he said he was. After leaving the hospital, Karl drove to the Bayshore but couldn't see the distinctive CKNW truck in the hotel's parking lot. "I phoned CKNW to see if there was any meeting that night anywhere, and there was none," said Karl. "I phoned the Bayshore, and there was no meeting there either. We went back to his house at 3:30 in the morning, and he never turned up. I phoned early in the morning, and he wasn't there. We knew he was a liar."

The Bayshore in the 1960s. (Vancouver Archives #1435-580)

Esther had her usual contingent of visitors the next day. Before heading to the hospital, Rene had swung by sales manager Mel Cooper's house to report on the BowMac promotion. "After discussing the promotion and some of the inconveniences of living in a car, we did discuss his wife's health, and he said that she was worse than he had first believed and that he thought it could be lead poisoning due to some type of spray-painting at the place where she worked," said Cooper. "I had brought up this subject because Rene had told Erm that they pretty nearly lost her." Cooper told Rene to take a couple more days off.

That night, after eating dinner, Esther's nausea and vomiting returned. "Her condition seemed to grow worse gradually, but she continued to try to eat and talked always of getting better and coming home to my house," said Mabel. "She seemed afraid to be left alone in the hospital room."

Dr Moscovitch had the hospital's chief dietician visit Esther to try to find some food that Esther could tolerate. "I even went as far as advising the family to try and bring in some choice food that she might like in order to get some food into her body," said Moscovitch. Rene would often stop by and help feed her at mealtimes, and it wasn't unusual for the nurses to see him bring her 7 Up, Tab, or her favourite milkshakes to drink.

Margie Scott and her mother visited Esther one evening after Esther had just returned from having a painful lumbar puncture and was being fed with an intravenous drip. "She sounded very low and depressed. She was unable to move her hands and feet—they seemed to be completely numb," says Scott. When Scott's mother held a glass of water for her, Esther took a sip but immediately vomited it back up and started to gag.

Esther had dropped twenty pounds (nine kilograms) and told her friends that she could no longer keep anything down. She constantly felt nauseated. Yet, "all things considered, she was really very bright and cheerful and laughing and joking and making the best of it," said Scott. "But she was very sick and couldn't turn over in bed, and when she wanted to be turned, the nurse had to do it for her. She couldn't move at all."

When the Scotts left, they saw Esther's mother with Sheila and Karl in the foyer. Mabel told Scott that doctors thought that Esther had contracted a virus in her nervous system. It could take between five months to a year for her to get over it. Mabel blamed Rene for not bringing in a specialist sooner. She told Scott that Rene didn't take any interest in his wife's condition, and that she had been checking up on Rene—and he wasn't where he claimed to be.

By June 19, Dr Moscovitch had to stop Esther's daily weigh-ins because she could no longer balance on the scale. "It got to the point where she was unable to sit up in a chair because of generalized pain in her legs and severe abdominal cramps," said head nurse Lydia Ratzlaff.

"She had muscular weakness and an acute sensitivity to touch. If we touched her skin at all she would cry out in pain. She literally had to be turned from side to side and have her limbs placed into proper alignment."

The movement of her limbs became uncoordinated. Her skin appeared dry and scaly. She had a blister-like rash on her chest and shoulders and down her arms. Nurses had stopped attempting to comb Esther's hair; it was just too distressing for her. They used ice packs to try to ease the agonizing pain in her neck.

The results of the tests for lead and paint poisoning had come back negative. The spinal fluid from the lumbar puncture showed an elevation of a protein factor that could indicate a viral infection.

In the meantime, Dr Moscovitch went to other specialists in the hospital. He called in Dr Beck, a specialist in hematology; Dr Buckler, the head of the physiotherapy department; and Dr Jones, a neurologist.

Dr Jones couldn't find anything in the history to suggest the cause of the numbness, but he noted that the muscles below Esther's elbows were completely paralyzed. The consensus was that Esther was suffering from an acute viral infection, and given time, she would recover. What most concerned Dr Moscovitch was that she had begun to have difficulty breathing and she was coughing up blood—symptoms that signalled impending heart failure. Moscovitch ordered blood transfusions, started her on steroids, and sent samples of her blood and stool to the virologist at the Provincial Department of Health. He was told he would have to wait up to four weeks for the results. Then Moscovitch had Esther transferred to a room that was closer to the nursing desk.

Margaret Robertson, the ward clerk, called Rene to tell him about the move. He told her he was pleased Esther was closer to the desk, and he hoped he would now be able to see more of his wife alone. "I told him that was fine, that we would tell the head nurse to pass word on to the afternoon shift to have Mrs Luond leave at ten p.m. that night." He said he would stay in the waiting room by the elevators until she was gone.

None of the nurses thought it was odd that Rene wanted to spend time alone with his wife. They saw him visit her every day; to outsiders they appeared quite happily married. Rene often stopped by the nurse's station to joke with them and bring them Riggio cigarettes and Coppertone suntan lotion from station promotions. All the nurses liked Rene—but in the '60s, when people tended to dress conservatively, they were puzzled by his clothes. "When I met Mr Castellani, I was surprised at the attire he was wearing," said Lydia Ratzlaff. "This consisted of a sweatshirt, Bermuda shorts, woollen socks, and running shoes. In conversation I asked him if he had been playing tennis. He said, 'No, this is my usual attire.'"

Registered nurse Evelyn Jackson also noticed Rene's casual dress. "One night, he was wearing shorts and made a remark to me that, 'You girls should be wearing bathing suits on duty.' I said it wouldn't look too professional."

Frank Iaci would often stop by in the afternoons to visit Esther and was shocked by her rapid deterioration. Esther told Frank that she knew her marriage was over. She wanted to get out of the hospital, take Jeannine, and live with her mother. Frank was fed up with Rene, and he decided to return that night and have it out with him about his girlfriend. "I told him I heard he was stepping out with another girl, and I thought he was carrying on rather badly and that he should not do what he was doing," he said. "I told him, 'Esther needs you desperately. Give her something worth coming out of hospital for.'"

Years before, Rene and Esther had had a falling-out with Frank when they found he was cheating on his wife. At the time, Frank had told them it was none of their business. Now Rene told Frank that there was no girlfriend, that it was all rumour. "I've worked hard at this job and got places," he told Frank. "He cut us all after that." Frank said. "I have never seen an individual so cold, so indifferent as Rene."

A few days after his talk with Frank Iaci, Rene was out helping Lolly look for a house. She was interested in a bungalow on Hoy Street in Vancouver, and on June 29, they met with Warren Peterson, the builder and owner, to negotiate a deal. There were a few things that needed work, and Rene told the builder that his future father-in-law would help him, as he was a cement finisher.

Lolly wrote up an interim receipt and put down a $100 deposit on the house. She asked that the mortgage application be put in her name. She told Peterson that they would be getting married in about two weeks and would be going on a holiday to Disneyland with their children for two weeks after that. "This gave about a month from the time they wrote this interim to the time they required possession of the house," said Peterson. He set up a meeting with a real estate agent named Allan Gillis.

Lolly introduced Rene as her fiancé, and Gillis asked them when they planned to be married. They told him in two to three weeks, and he suggested it would be better to put the house in her married name because it was difficult to get a mortgage in a woman's name. Gillis told them it would also save legal costs later if they wanted to change the title to the married name. "They thought that was a good idea, and on the basis of that, I put the application in the name of Adelaide Anne Castellani and Rene Emile Castellani." Gillis told them he would inspect the property and, if all was well, file the application with the bank asking for a loan of $11,000 over twenty years at seven percent interest.

Gillis wrote up Rene's occupation as radio broadcaster and Lolly's as housewife. School had finished for the summer, and Jeannine was now staying with her aunt Gloria and uncle Bud Foxgord and their three daughters in their big house on Drummond Street in Point Grey. Rene would drop by the Foxgords' for dinner fairly frequently, but if he wasn't working or at the hospital, he was at Lolly's. He told Mrs Defries, the nursing supervisor, that he wasn't living at home. He gave the nurses a phone number where they could reach him when he was not at work.

Esther Castellani spent the last seven weeks of her life at Vancouver General Hospital. (Vancouver Archives #2008-022.0731102)

CHAPTER 11

SERIOUSLY ILL

By the end of June, Dr Moscovitch had become extremely concerned about Esther's deteriorating health. The small red rash that she had on admittance to hospital had spread over her whole body and developed pustules that had become infected. Her kidneys were shutting down, she had progressive heart failure and severe diarrhea, and she had started to pour out protein in her urine, pus, and blood cells.

"The poor woman could not eat for many weeks of her stay. She had to be fed by a vein. She was given many, many medications to support her general condition," noted Moscovitch, who, though worried, was still optimistic. "She was a very courageous girl, and at all times she kept asking when she could go home. Her outlook at all times was good. I grant you she was so uncomfortable by virtue of her symptoms, but basically her emotional status was excellent."

Her caloric intake was not. She was averaging 766 calories a day. On June 30, her chart noted that she had custard from home and consumed 701 calories, and by early July this had dropped to 500.

In early July, Dr Moscovitch asked Dr Jones, the neurologist, for another consult. Jones agreed with Moscovitch that the most likely cause of Esther's troubles was a viral infection and anticipated a slow improvement in her condition. But by July 5, she had reached the point where she needed blood transfusions to address anemia, and Moscovitch told the family that anything they could do to tempt her to eat would be welcome.

Mabel, who visited Esther every evening after she finished work and every afternoon when she wasn't working, cooked up some ground round steak and green beans that Esther had always liked. It was too late to give it to her that night, so the nurses put it in the fridge for the next day. When Sheila arrived to visit Esther, she found Rene trying to feed his wife her mother's warmed-up cooking. The room was stifling hot and Esther looked completely worn out.

Sheila told him to stop and try again when she was more comfortable and relaxed. Esther told her that she didn't want any more of the food, that she didn't like the taste of it. There was a glass of milk on the tray. "He kept the spoon in front of her mouth, for one thing, and he was sort of shoving it at her," said Sheila. "And she tried again, but she said, no, it was nauseating her, and she didn't want to eat it."

When he didn't stop trying to coax her to eat, Esther became upset. Sheila took the bowl out of his hand and put it on the table beside her. "She looked so dreadful, and she told me that there had been a doctor or someone in examining her, and it left her exhausted. She just looked completely played out," said Sheila.

Rene then told her that if Esther wasn't going to eat the food, Sheila should flush it down the toilet, as it would make her mother happy to think she'd eaten something. "I finally took it and did it to shut him up," said Sheila. "When the nurse saw the empty bowl, she said, 'Oh, good girl, you have eaten your dinner up,' and Rene said, 'Yes, pretty good, eh?' And I was disturbed by this, because they were keeping a very close watch of every intake she had. I followed the nurse into the hall to tell her that Esther had not eaten it at all—it was thrown out—because I was afraid they might think she had this nourishment."

When Sheila saw Rene outside the room a little later she asked him if he knew anything about the causes of Esther's illness and whether there was anything the doctors may not have told the rest of the family. "He said, 'When a house burns down, I don't look for where the fire started, I look for where I can build a new one,'" said Sheila. "Then he said, "Well, the doctor doesn't phone me. He doesn't tell me anything. I don't know anything.'"

Friends and family were encouraged to bring food into the hospital to tempt Esther to eat and drink. (Vancouver Archives #2008-022.076)

Even though she was in pain and suffering horribly, Sheila said that Esther was always cheerful and optimistic and talked about going back to work. "It was hard to converse with her because she was obviously so sick," said Sheila. "Yet she believed she was coming home again."

The next day, Esther began bringing up pink, frothy sputum—an indicator of heart failure—and gasping for breath. Her lips and finger-nails turned blue. For the first time in her seven-week hospital stay, Moscovitch became really worried and put Esther on the seriously ill list. He notified her husband and gave orders to put her in an oxygen tent. The nurses had to move her frequently, because she was restless and couldn't move her limbs.

Joyce Dayton visited Esther that night and was distressed to see that even with the oxygen, she was still having trouble breathing. "I was only allowed to stay about five minutes and she said hello and seemed to slip into almost a sleep. I guess seeing me reminded her about the store and she said, 'I will put it aside for you,' and that is the last thing she said to me."

Early in the morning of July 11, Rene, who was dressed in his typical hospital attire—track suit and running shoes—phoned his sister-in-law from the hospital. "Sheila, you better keep the old lady away from here," he told her. "It is pretty bad. I guess it is the end." Sheila told him that she couldn't keep Esther's mother away, and she would come to the hospital right away. Minutes later, while two nurses were turning her around in bed, Esther died. Dr Moscovitch was notified at 10:17 a.m. and pronounced the time of death at 10:25 a.m.

Although Esther had refused to see a priest while she was alive, after her death, Lorenzo Gelinas performed the last rites with Rene, Dr Moscovitch, and nurse Jean Nichol in attendance.

Sheila and Karl then arrived at the hospital, followed by Frank Iaci and Gloria. Esther's mother, who became hysterical on hearing the news of her daughter's death, was taken to emergency and sedated.

"I didn't feel I could sign the death warrant," said Dr Moscovitch. "I informed her husband I would require an autopsy to determine the cause of death."

CHAPTER 12

DISNEYLAND

According to Sheila Luond, after Dr Moscovitch told Rene that he wanted an autopsy performed, Rene said to him, "Oh, Barney, don't! Don't talk to me now. I can't think about it now." Moscovitch thought that Rene's reaction was to be expected, considering that his wife had just died, and asked him to think it over and let him know as soon as possible.

Rene phoned Margie Scott from the hospital to tell her that Esther had died. He told her that he was going to pick Jeannine up at his sister's house and break the news of her mother's death. He wanted to come by for Cocoa because Jeannine would want to see her dog.

Rene and Jeannine drove to the Scotts' in North Vancouver, and Rene made several phone calls from the kitchen. "He was quite calm, but he seemed to be very tired and slightly dazed," said Scott. "He said he had not slept for two or three days. Because the child was present, Esther's death was never mentioned, and we just carried on the best we could and tried not to be emotional."

"I remember him coming in and saying, 'Jeannine, I have to go to the hospital,' and I was so excited. I said, 'You're going to bring my mum home today, aren't you?' and I remember him saying something like, 'Oh, we'll see,' but he didn't let on that anything was wrong," recalls Jeannine. "Then he said, 'I have something to tell you,' and he said, 'Your mum's going to heaven.' Just like that. And then he said, 'She told me to tell you to take care of me.'"

He told Scott that he'd be taking Jeannine on a trip to California after the funeral. She told him it was a good idea to get away, and she would happily take care of their dog again while they were gone.

A visitor at Disneyland, mid-1960s. (Courtesy Kate Bird)

Then Rene and Jeannine got back in the CKNW truck and drove to Esther's parents' house.

"When we were driving down the street, I remember just sitting there looking at him," says Jeannine. "He was all I had. I was so dependent on him. It wouldn't matter what he said. If he'd said the sky was green, I would have said, 'Oh yeah, looks good.' Then he started talking to me about Lolly, the lady at work. He said she had a little boy, and he asked me how I felt about going to Disneyland to get away from everything."

A few hours later, the family and Frank Iaci gathered at the Luonds' home. Rene called Bill Hughes to tell him Esther had died. Hughes asked him about the cause of death, and when Rene told him that they weren't sure, he asked him if there would be an autopsy. Rene told him that he wasn't going to consent to one. "I said, 'Well, Rene, I think for medical science and for the people who follow that, it would be interesting to know why your wife died.'"

When Rene got off the phone, Frank told him that if he didn't consent, it would look suspicious, and the court would probably order an autopsy. Rene phoned Dr Moscovitch to tell him that he would be down shortly to sign the papers to allow one.

That night, Mel Cooper dropped in to Rene's Kerrisdale duplex to offer his condolences. He found Rene and Jeannine watching television in the living room. Rene had his feet up on the chesterfield, laughing at a comedian on *The Ed Sullivan Show*. He told Cooper that he was going to Disneyland with his daughter, and they'd start fresh; they had a new life to begin.

Cooper was there for about three hours and stayed while Rene took several phone calls. "Jeannine seemed quite composed, and she did not cry nor appear as though she had been crying. Rene would say, 'Mummy is a lot better off now.' Jeannine talked about going to Disneyland. Rene talked some business, and I changed the subject. I couldn't believe that Rene could have suffered such a great loss and be so casual. It did not strike me as a normal reaction."

The next day, Rene came into the station. "We all thought he was taking it so well," said Cooper. Glen Garvin, Rene's immediate boss, told Rene they could swap vehicles so that he and Jeannine could take his new Chevrolet station wagon to California, with the CKNW logo displayed prominently on the side.

Later that day, Rene took Jeannine to the funeral home to select a casket for her mother. "I remember the dim lights in the funeral parlour," says Jeannine. "I chose a gold-coloured casket with satin on the inside. Then we went back to the house on 41st because he wanted me to choose something for her to wear. I chose a powder-blue skirt and a jacket that buttoned up that she loved to wear. She probably bought it at Hills of Kerrisdale. I had a powder-blue rosary, and I wanted her to have that with her."

On the day before Esther's funeral, Rene phoned Wally Garrett, a friend and the announcer he had worked with during the BowMac promotion. Rene knew that Wally's brother Marshall and sister-in-law Florence ran the Kona Kai Motel in Anaheim, and Rene asked him if he could get him a deal. He told him that he needed to take his daughter away from everything for a few days. Garrett was happy to help.

Children were not allowed to attend Esther's funeral, so Jeannine stayed with her uncle Bud and her cousins for the day.

After the funeral, Rene went to see Esther's parents and told them that he and Jeannine would be leaving for Disneyland the next day. "He had the station wagon from CKNW," said Mabel. "He said he had sleeping bags, and the station had arranged time off so he could take Jeannine to Disneyland. And we were rather pleased about that. He was always like my son, let's face it. I called him my son all the time." Mabel gave Jeannine some spending money, and Gloria slipped out into the laneway behind the house and handed Rene some cash for the trip.

The day after Esther's funeral, Rene and Lolly kept their appointment with Barbara Tamburri, the assistant accountant at the Canadian Imperial Bank of Commerce. Tamburri took a statement of their employment, salary, and assets. Almost all of the assets, including a one-year-old Volvo, were in Lolly Miller's name. Rene exaggerated his annual salary to $7,600 and added his record collection, amplifier, and furniture that he valued at $3,000. But when Tamburri ran a credit check, she found that Rene's rating was poor, and she told Gillis, the real estate agent, that even though their combined financial picture looked good, based on Rene's credit rating, the bank was unwilling to proceed with the mortgage.

"Mr Castellani phoned me about an hour later and said there were extenuating circumstances regarding his financial and credit picture and would I reconsider," said Tamburri. Rene told her that he had been a partner and manager of the Willows Hotel in Campbell River when four people lost their lives in the fire that destroyed it. He felt morally responsible for their deaths, had been under a doctor's care for about a year, and couldn't work. Tamburri felt that this was a reasonable explanation and told Rene that they would proceed with the mortgage on the strength of Lolly Miller's assets and credit rating. The loan application would be made out in the joint names of Rene Emile and Adelaide Ann Castellani. Because they were not yet married, she told them that she would require proof of marriage before the bank would advance any funds.

The letter to the Kinross Mortgage Corporation from CIBC manager R.S. Keyes that accompanied the loan application read:

> The credit report that we received from the Vancouver Credit Bureau on Mr Rene E. Castellani was very poor showing county court writs and collection bills now paid. While part owner and manager of the Willows Hotel in Campbell River the hotel burned down and there were a number of people killed. This affected Mr Castellani as he felt it was his responsibility and he was put under doctor's care for more than a year and could not work. They were living on his wife's income during this period and their finances became quite involved. Castellani now appears to be making good progress and should experience no difficulty in meeting the monthly mortgage payments. He has just recently remarried and as indicated in their statement, most of the assets are in her name. Payments will be made by way of pre-authorized debits through Mrs Castellani's savings account at our Kingsway and Willingdon, Burnaby, branch. We feel the covenant is first class and as there is ample protection for a loan of $11,000 we are pleased to add our recommendation.

The day after Esther's funeral, Rene and Lolly applied for a mortgage in their new married names. (From inquest documents)

The new family of four spent the night at a motel in Burnaby and left for California early the next morning. That same morning, Glen Garvin was heading to work when he saw his station wagon going south. "The Fraser Street Bridge opened, and we were all piled up in traffic, and when it began to move again I recognized my station wagon, and I recognized Rene in his red sweatshirt." Garvin could see a woman in the passenger seat, but couldn't make out who it was, and at least two children bobbing in the back seat. When he got to the station, he asked Mel Cooper if Rene had relatives going with him to California. Cooper didn't know, but they discussed Rene's strange calmness at his wife's funeral.

The new family stopped at the Sea Lion Caves in Oregon and visited the Redwood National Park in northern California. Jeannine

Promotional photo of Rene Castellani. He signed it "To Toad," one of the pet names he had for Lolly Miller.

remembers spending a couple of nights in different motels along the way. Rene and Lolly took the main bed, and she and Don slept on the pullout.

Esther was never mentioned again. "We didn't talk about it," says Jeannine. "We were on to our new life. He had me look at how fun it is going to be, how wonderful it is going to be. And I thought, I guess it is. He was very manipulative. I don't know how Donnie felt about him. He was quite a bit younger." Lolly's son was five at the time.

When they got to the Anaheim motel, Rene introduced Lolly to the Garretts as his sister, which they thought was odd. The four tourists stayed in a room with a double bed and a double rollaway bed, which was put in for their visit. The motel register showed that they had booked in as Mr and Mrs Castellani of 2509 West 41st in Vancouver, Canada.

"I never really got a chance to grieve my mum," says Jeannine. "I was swooped up and off we went to Disneyland, and then I had a new mummy. It was just so weird. I just had to shut it off because they did. There was no husband that was distraught over losing his wife. I just never saw that."

The day after Esther died, her body was delivered to the morgue at Vancouver General Hospital to be autopsied.

CHAPTER 13
OMBUDSMAN OF THE DEAD

At the hospital morgue, senior pathologist Dr David Hardwick assigned Esther's post-mortem to his trainee Dr Frank Anderson, who was to be assisted by George Beaumont, the morgue attendant. Anderson noted the case number as A-65-428 (A for autopsy, 65 for the year, and 428 for the 428th autopsy performed that year) and checked the identification: Esther Castellani, a forty-year-old female, weighing 160 pounds (72.5 kilograms) and measuring 65.5 inches (166 centimetres) long.

After Anderson examined the outside of her body, Beaumont made a Y-shaped incision starting from the shoulder joints so that Anderson could examine the chest, the thorax, and the rest of the body. He removed the lungs, heart, liver, spleen, kidneys, genital organs, and gastrointestinal tract, weighing each organ and cutting it open to inspect its interior. He then cut sections from these and put them in a jar containing formalin solution. He took pieces of heart, liver, and kidney and placed them in a small sterile jar and stored these in the deep freezer. Then he put the organs, in plastic bags, back into the body cavities.

Next, Anderson opened the skull to examine the brain, which he removed and placed in a receptacle containing formalin. Returning to the body, he noted that the lungs were filled with fluid and blood—a condition called pulmonary edema—consistent with heart failure, but otherwise, her heart, lungs, and other organs appeared normal. Anderson told Dr Moscovitch that although heart disease was the mode of death, he still had no idea what had caused it.

Esther Castellani had been one of the more frustrating cases that Moscovitch had ever treated. He had hoped the autopsy would shed

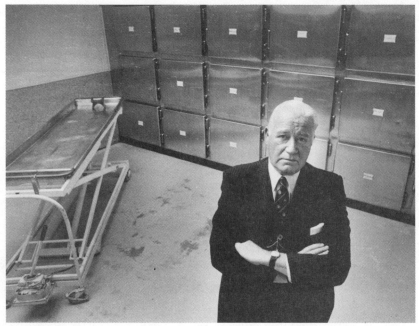

Glen McDonald was Vancouver's coroner from 1954 to 1980. (Photo by Steve Bosch, courtesy *Vancouver Sun*, October 28, 1979)

light on the cause of her long illness. He had also liked Esther and spent much of the last seven weeks trying to heal her. He often saw her twice in one day. He had brought in seven different specialists to consult on her case and performed more than 120 tests. He wasn't ready to let it go.

Dr Moscovitch went home and spent the next few hours poring over Esther's medical history, looking for anything that he might have missed that could explain the cause of death. "As a matter of fact, I rewrote the whole history, along with her clinical course and all her laboratory investigations—everything," he said. "I realized that this woman had a gross assault not on one organ alone but on many systems of her body. True, she died of heart disease, but she had involvement of her gastrointestinal tract, her blood, her kidneys, her spleen, her nervous system, and I asked myself what condition, what disease, could possibly give rise to such a multiple system involvement?"

The myriad tests performed on Esther while she was alive confirmed that she did not have diabetes or any form of rare neurological or connective tissue diseases. Blood tests had indicated that she might have been suffering from the effects of some type of toxin but had ruled out lead, the most likely metal to cause this kind of reaction. "I went into a study of the various elements that a person can become exposed to in a lifetime— there's about fifteen of them—and I realized that arsenic was a possibility," said Dr Moscovitch.

Arsenic would explain not only the nausea and vomiting but also the numbness and tingling sensation in her fingers and toes.[17] He also noted uneasily that it was easy to miss a case of chronic arsenic poisoning in which the victim died from repeated small doses because symptoms closely mimicked those of influenza and acute gastroenteritis. He knew from his research that arsenic trioxide had been used as an effective way to dispatch an inconvenient relative or co-worker in the 1700s and throughout the 1800s because it was odourless and, except for a slight metallic flavour; virtually tasteless; dissolved fairly easily; and looked like flour or sugar. It was also found in paints, wallpaper, fabrics, soaps, and spring water, and it was cheap and easy to get because it was a common ingredient in household insecticides and pesticides.

Like most of his contemporaries, Dr Moscovitch had never come across a case of murder by arsenic poisoning, but when he started

---

17 The World Health Organization notes that "the immediate symptoms of acute arsenic poisoning include vomiting, abdominal pain and diarrhoea. These are followed by numbness and tingling of the extremities, muscle cramping and death, in extreme cases." *World Health Organization*, "Arsenic Fact Sheet," http://www.who.int/en/news-room/fact-sheets/detail/arsenic.

practising medicine in the 1930s, arsenic had been used to treat syphilis. "I got to know something about arsenic and its effect on the body," he said. More recently, he had treated workers who had inhaled arsine in an industrial accident. He told Dr Hardwick his theory and asked that he send some of the tissue samples to the city analyst for investigation.

Ted Fennell had been appointed city analyst in 1949, the year that J.F.C.B. Vance, once known as Vancouver's Sherlock Holmes, had retired. Fennell told Hardwick that the lab would run toxicology tests on the tissue samples, looking specifically for arsenic, and they would be handled by their chemist, Alexander J. Beaton.

Beaton analyzed a mixture of small sections of heart, liver, and kidney, and a section of the brain, using the Gutzeit test, a common test for the detection of arsenic at the time. Traces of arsenic are naturally present in the human body—on average about .03 parts per million—but the amounts that Beaton discovered were completely off the charts. He found that the mixed tissue of heart, liver, and kidney contained 24 parts per million of arsenic—roughly 800 times more then he should find. This result was so high, in fact, that he immediately tested the formalin solution used in the hospital to make sure that George Beaumont, the morgue attendant, hadn't used arsenic instead of calcium to stabilize the formaldehyde.

Beaton mailed his findings to Dr Hardwick and went on holiday, leaving the investigation in the hands of Eldon Rideout, assistant city analyst. Now that Esther's death had turned from a medical inquiry into a possible homicide, it was time to involve the coroner, Judge Glen McDonald.

McDonald called himself the Ombudsman of the Dead. He told people it was his job to find the cause of death in order to help the living, and he did this from his morgue on East Cordova Street, where an average of 1,100 bodies passed through each year. He smoked fifty cigarettes a day, drank beer and spirits kept beside forensic specimens in an office fridge, and conducted one or two inquests a week that looked into deaths ranging from shootings and stabbings to drug overdoses and traffic accidents.

His job was to assemble a jury and determine whether death was natural, accidental, suicide, or homicide. After he retired in 1980, he admitted to occasionally lying to priests so that his Catholic victims could be buried in consecrated ground. "I'd say we hadn't yet reached a conclusion," he told a *Vancouver Sun* reporter in 1992. The funeral would go ahead as if the death was not a suicide, and McDonald would sign the death certificate when the body was safely in the ground.

This was the first case of arsenic poisoning that McDonald had seen since he was appointed coroner in 1954. The first thing he did was install himself in the science section of the Vancouver Public Library and read everything he could find about arsenic poisoning. As he wrote in his autobiography, *How Come I'm Dead?*, he had the feeling that Rene Castellani had been at the library some months before, doing exactly the same thing.

McDonald noted that arsenic is a heavy metal found in common items such as insecticides and pesticides. It is toxic to the gastrointestinal tract. Doctors once called arsenic poisoning gastric fever because symptoms include nausea, vomiting, abdominal pain, and diarrhea. Other signs are hair loss and numbness. Hemorrhage from the intestine and loss of fluids cause vascular collapse, resulting in dizziness, convulsions, coma, and death. Arsenic, he read, is deposited in the hair, fingernails, and skin and can be detected years later in exhumed bodies. "Arsenic poisoning is something we rarely find today, although at the turn of the century there was frequent use of the poison in murders. It was used a lot for killing rats and mice as well as humans, as many famous old Scotland Yard cases testify," wrote McDonald in *How Come I'm Dead?*

As was his power under the Cemeteries Act, McDonald advised the Attorney General and arranged to have Esther's newly buried body exhumed. Then he notified the police about the next day's exhumation. They were now treating the death as a homicide.

Staff Sergeant Bill Porteous of the Vancouver Police Department (VPD) was put in charge and assigned homicide detectives Alex Reid and Archie McKay to investigate the death of Esther Castellani. Early on the morning of August 3, 1965, McDonald, Reid, McKay, as well as staff from the lab arrived at Forest Lawn Memorial Park in Burnaby armed with shovels and grub hoes. They gathered around the grave that held Esther Castellani's body and proceeded to dig up the casket that had been placed there only three weeks before. The men stowed it in the back of the black wagon and drove to the morgue, where pathologist Dr Thomas Redo Harmon would perform a second, more extensive post-mortem.

News of the exhumation shocked Esther's already devastated family. They gathered at the Luonds' home that night. Esther's mother couldn't believe that her son-in-law had murdered her daughter, but Gloria did. She said, "I thought all the way along it was Rene."

Then the bank notified Rene that his and Lolly's mortgage application had been turned down. The official reason given was that the house "was poorly sited and the location could only be described as fair." But the more likely reason was that Esther's death had hit the front page of the newspapers, with mentions of arsenic and murder.

Rene had gone back to work at CKNW after his return from Disneyland. "It was around the beginning of August that I heard that Rene's wife had died of arsenic poisoning," said Mel Cooper. "He made no comment about this. Once, he said his in-laws were saying things that were upsetting him. I said, 'Rene, what do you think happened?' He said, 'I have no idea. I don't know.'"

But what Rene must have known is that as soon as the cause of death changed from natural causes to homicide, as the husband, he would be suspect number one.

The Castellani family moved into 2509 West 41st Avenue on April 1, 1965, a few months before Esther's death. (Photo by Eve Lazarus, 2018)

CHAPTER 14
THE POLICE INVESTIGATE

The first interview on detectives Reid and McKay's list was Esther's husband, Rene.

Their married life was normal, he told them, though they had the usual arguments. "She beefed about my long hours. We were in debt before she went into hospital and had to stop working. She had no insurance. It had been dropped years ago. We couldn't afford the payments."

It was a tough time, he said, because both his parents had been in Vancouver General Hospital that Christmas, and his eighty-three-year-old father, who had been dealing with senility, had ultimately died from a heart attack and a bleeding gastric ulcer on March 7. Rene's mother, who was also in poor health, continued to live with his sister, Louise.

After a couple of hours of questioning, Reid and McKay drove Rene home and told him they'd like to search the place. Rene told them to go ahead. Reid looked in the cupboard under the kitchen sink. The small space was packed with ordinary household items, including a bottle of Windex, Glide dishwashing liquid, Bon Ami cleaner, scuff pads, a shoeshine kit, a garbage pail, and a can of Ortho Triox, a weed killer clearly marked as poison with a skull and crossbones on the label.

"I brought this can out and asked Castellani if he had seen it before, and he said, 'I've never seen it before.' Then he said, 'I thought it was a can of lighter fluid for the charcoal barbecue.' We opened the can and it looked to be about an inch and a half down from the top."

It was their first break. Rene many have been many things, but judging by the state of the backyard, he wasn't a gardener. They found no spraying instruments around the house or evidence that weed killer had been sprayed. And Ortho Triox was an odd choice for a residential garden. It was a strong herbicide that would kill not only weeds but also the lawn and everything else on it.

Rene's landlord, Robert Carney, told them that he had the duplex cleaned out before the Castellanis moved in. He thought everything had been removed, he said, but couldn't be sure that an item such as the can of Ortho Triox wasn't overlooked. The previous tenant, he said, had moved and didn't leave a forwarding address.

The detectives collected up the household items and put them in a cardboard carton.

Next, they hoped to learn more about the Castellanis' marriage from a close friend of Esther's: Margie Scott. Scott told them she and her husband had lived next door to the Castellanis for about eighteen months, and the two families had become very friendly. She had stayed friends with Esther after they moved, and they had been in frequent contact. The investigation got a lot more interesting when Scott told them that Esther had confided in her that Rene was having an affair and that she had confronted him about it. She'd also been getting anonymous phone calls late at night from a woman asking if she knew her husband was going around with someone named Lolly. Rene had told Esther that it was all just gossip, but she hadn't believed him, Scott told the detectives, and the marriage had continued to deteriorate.

Since Esther had confronted Rene in October with the letter she had found in his wallet signed "Love, Lolly," things had never been right between them, Scott said. Esther had told her friend that when she asked her husband why he was no longer interested in her, he told her that he wasn't interested in women anymore.

Rene had phoned the Scotts the day after Esther's funeral, on July 14, and asked if they could look after their dog and hamster while he and Jeannine were in California. The next time Scott saw him was on

July 30. "Last Friday, Rene came to see us after supper at 7:30 p.m. He said he had a friend with a sick cat," said Scott. "My husband and I went down, and Rene introduced his friend, a Lolly Miller. She had her little boy with her, a little blond boy of four or five. I realized who she was, and we said nothing, and we managed to carry it off. My husband looked at the animal and decided to keep it in for treatment, and we had a few words and they left." Lolly, Scott told them, had picked up the cat earlier that day.

At this point, Esther had been dead for less than three weeks.

Detectives Reid and McKay had four family members and friends of Esther Castellani lined up to interview the next day, but it was beginning to feel like the age-old story of married man meets younger woman and murders inconvenient wife. And it was probably no coincidence, thought the detectives, that Esther started getting sick just after she confronted her husband about his mistress.

The first interview scheduled by Reid and McKay was at 11:10 the next morning with Esther's younger sister. Gloria told them that the first time she had seen Esther in a while was that April when they were both visiting their mother. "Rene and Jeannine came in, and after they left I mentioned to my mother that Esther did not look well as her face was puffy and distorted," she said. "I had never seen her looking this bad. My mother told me that she had been unwell and short of breath, and I said she looked as though she had been poisoned."

Later, Gloria said she phoned Esther at home and asked if she could do anything for her. Esther said she wanted some Jell-O. Gloria went out, bought the packages of Jell-O, and made it up in Esther's kitchen. "There was no stove, only a small hot plate," she said. "Esther was on the chesterfield in the living room. She had a cover on her, and she couldn't get up. Jeannine was there. I told her that I didn't understand her taking pills, as she had not been tested for anything. She said she was being treated for ulcers, then gallbladder."

The detectives next went to the home of Esther's sister-in-law Sheila Luond. They'd known each other for more than sixteen years, Sheila told the detectives, and she gave them a recap of Esther's illness. Even though she had been ill for a number of months, Esther had been "excited and happy" to move into the new duplex. And when Sheila and Esther's brother, Karl, dropped by with a present for Esther's birthday in March, they found the Castellanis in the process of moving to their new place.

Later, they visited them at the new house. "Esther and Rene appeared to be getting along well," she said. About ten days later, when they dropped in to visit Esther, Rene, and Jeannine, Esther appeared listless "and not herself. But I wasn't concerned about her. I thought she was overtired from the move and everything," said Sheila.

The Castellanis' long-time friend Frank Iaci was next on the interview list. The detectives thought that he might side with Rene but were surprised when he opened up about Rene's affair. Iaci told them that he had been shocked; he would never have suspected Rene of playing around on his wife. Iaci had returned to Vancouver from Las Vegas in March 1965. Esther told Frank that Rene had said the affair was over, but she didn't sound convinced. After that, Frank's friendship with Rene cooled.

"I had heard that there had been something taking place with another woman, but I got home, and we went for our Sunday drives, and things seemed to be all right," Iaci told the detectives. "Then she got real sick, and we didn't see so much of one another, and they didn't come down to the restaurant. They used to be down all the time on Friday or Saturday nights and sit around and help if we needed it. I was really fond of Esther. Esther is perfection as far as I am concerned."

Rene Castellani was now the prime suspect, and Reid and McKay decided to turn up the heat the following day. Unable to find him at his home or work, they phoned his brother-in-law Bud Foxgord to find out where he was. Foxgord told them Rene was out for dinner with Lolly and Jeannine and he would leave a message for Rene to phone the detectives.

A little before 7:30 p.m., Rene phoned the detectives and told them he was now at his home. They arrived at the duplex on West 41st just over half an hour later. Rene told them that just he and Jeannine had gone to dinner at White Spot, but he admitted that he had a girlfriend named Lolly who used to work at CKNW. She'd left the station in May to look after her little boy, he told them. Lolly reminded him of Esther, he said, and they were talking about getting married.

"You told us your family life was all right," Detective Reid told him. "You know what people will think if you have a girlfriend and your wife dies of arsenic [poisoning]? "

Rene answered, "Do you think I'm stupid enough that I would give her anything that could be traced, Detective Reid?"

Reid asked Rene if he thought Esther had committed suicide because her marriage was breaking up. He seemed shocked by the question. "God forbid. I wouldn't think this girl would be the type who would take her life."

Rene then handed the detectives a bill for thirty-seven dollars from a gardener for work he had done on June 17, 1965, just over seven weeks before. A call to the gardener confirmed that no weed killer had been used on the garden on the day he cleaned up the yard. He also told the detectives that he hadn't yet been paid.

Rene told the detectives that Jeannine had mentioned that Esther poured something on the weeds in the garden. "You can ask her," he told them. They didn't ask Jeannine, but Detective Reid collected some weeds with withered brown leaves to give to the assistant city analyst Eldon Rideout to test for arsenic. The analyst found the level within the range expected for untreated soil—meaning the weeds and dandelions in the Castellanis' backyard had not received any of the missing Ortho Triox. Had they asked Jeannine, she might have told them that the closest her mother ever came to gardening was spraying herself with the White Shoulders perfume she loved—it smelled of her favourite flowers: lily of the valley and lilac.

Soon after the interview, Rene retained Albert Mackoff as his lawyer, who told police that Rene would no longer discuss the death of his wife with the police or anyone else.

The detectives then decided to take a closer look at Lolly. They found that she and Rene had applied for a mortgage to buy a house on Vancouver's East Side. Allan Gillis, their realtor, told the detectives that Rene and Lolly had come to his office in June to apply for a mortgage on a house on Hoy Street. Lolly had wanted the house to be in her name, but when Gillis learned that they planned to be married in a few weeks, he suggested they apply for a joint mortgage in their married names.

Barbara Tamburri from the bank confirmed that Rene and Lolly had told her they were to be married. The bank had originally turned down their loan application because of Rene's poor credit rating but later changed their mind. "He said his wife was the one working at the time, and he was under doctor's care for about one year. The bills fell behind, and his wife got tired of carrying the load and started charging all over town," Tamburri told them. "Now he had a fine girl with assets and he was going to start a new life."

He hadn't told Tamburri the name of the doctor who'd ostensibly treated him, and the bank had not checked, she said. If the bank had checked, they would also have discovered that his depression that, according to Rene, stopped him from finding steady employment hadn't stopped him from performing at clubs around town and launching the Attic coffee house. The bank processed the applications based on Lolly's assets and Rene's employment with CKNW. Rene and Lolly had brought their children to the bank and told Tamburri they were on their way to Disneyland.

Neither Tamburri nor Gillis had any idea that at the time Rene applied for the mortgage he was still married to someone else.

As the detectives began digging into Lolly's past, they found that before moving back in with her mother and stepfather, she had rented a basement suite from Ronald and Sylvia Smail on Kincaid Street. Smail told the detectives that he and his wife became friends with Lolly when they were living on the same floor in an apartment building in Burnaby. Later, when they bought a house, they asked Lolly if she was interested in renting their basement suite. Lolly brought Rene to look at the suite before she decided to rent it. She and Rene painted the kitchen, and then he helped her and Don move in, in February 1965.

Rene, said Smail, was a frequent visitor and often had to be asked to move the CKNW truck when it was parked in the Smails' lane, blocking their garage. When Lolly brought Rene upstairs to visit, they had talked about Rene's impending divorce; in fact, they were surprised to learn that he was still married. Sylvia Smail told detectives that when Lolly rented the basement suite, she worked days on the weekends and the four p.m. to midnight shift during the week. "I used to see the truck in the daytime," she said. "We were under the impression that he had got a divorce in June 1965. Lolly led me to believe that."

The detectives were looking forward to meeting Lolly. They arrived at her parents' Burnaby house at 9:30 p.m. and were taken to her basement suite. Don was in bed, and Lolly's mother, Augie Giuliani, stayed throughout the interview.

Lolly told Reid and McKay that she had been employed at CKNW from March 1962 to May 1965 and had known Rene since 1964.

"Have you ever heard of [Esther Castellani] receiving anonymous phone calls?" asked Reid. "Some woman phoned Esther and said, 'I want your husband and I'm going to get him.'"

"There were quite a few anonymous phone calls around CKNW and also gossip about Rene," replied Lolly.

The detectives already knew that Rene was a frequent visitor to Lolly's basement suite but were interested in what she would say. As they expected, she denied it and told them he had only been there on a couple of work-related visits and there had been some misunderstandings among her co-workers. For example, one night in late April 1964, she and three other women from the station had thrown a surprise wedding shower for a colleague. Rene had come to take photos, made some punch for the women, and then left around 6:30 p.m. There was nothing else to it, she told them.

The next time he came over was during a snowfall that November. He picked up Lolly and Gina Steeves, a secretary at CKNW, and took them to work. "This caused talk around the station," Lolly told Reid. "Someone said Rene's truck was there at three in the morning. Erm Fiorillo talked to me about this. The truck was there, but Rene wasn't. He had borrowed my car."

When Rene brought Lolly's Volvo back the next day, she made him coffee. Her mistake, she told detectives, was mentioning it to Maureen Stoney, the woman she'd thrown the surprise shower for. "I happened to mention that Rene was up for coffee," said Lolly. "Apparently she went to Rene and said, 'My, you are getting pretty chummy.'"

Another time, he helped her stepfather move some furniture, she said. She knew Rene was married, and there was no romance attached to these visits. Reid and McKay didn't believe a word of it. "Mrs Castellani's sickness was showing up at Christmas or by New Year's, or even before that. Did you have any associations with him then?" asked Reid.

Lolly told him they'd occasionally talk when they saw each other at the station, and once he asked her where he could get some loud pyjamas and a nightcap to wear while he was doing the BowMac promotion. She told him that her mother could make these items for him. "We gave him the bill and got paid," she said.

"Did he tell you when his wife went into the hospital?" asked Reid.

"I can't remember when it was, but I heard she was in there," Lolly answered.

"Did you inquire about his wife?"

"I probably asked, but I wouldn't pry because it might upset a person."

"Did he ever tell you what he thought was wrong with Esther?"

"No. The only one I heard him talking about was Jeannine," she said

The detectives asked about the house that she had tried to buy on Hoy Street. Lolly told them that she had received $25,000, in instalments, after the death of her husband in 1962, but because she was presently unemployed, she needed to have a co-signer. She told the detectives that she was shocked when she and Rene visited the bank and found they had filed a mortgage application in the names Rene Castellani and Adelaide Castellani. Lolly said that they didn't form a relationship until after the trip to Disneyland in July. "Rene had decided that he was going to take Jeannine away from this, and she asked Don and I to go with them to Disneyland," said Lolly.

"Jeannine said that her mother wouldn't want us to go around crying. Jeannine, I believe, had prepared herself for her mother's death."

When the detective asked if she was now in a serious relationship with Rene, she told him that, yes, they now planned to be married after the inquest was over.

Reid told her that the inquest would reveal that Esther was murdered. "Have you any thoughts about who would give Esther the arsenic?" he asked her.

"I don't know," said Lolly. "Who would?"

CHAPTER 15
BACK AT THE MORGUE

While the VPD's homicide department was carefully building a case against Rene, determining his motive for murder and the means, scientists at the city analyst's lab were investigating Esther's cause of death, and Dr Harmon was preparing to perform a second post-mortem at the city morgue.

Dr Harmon opened the casket and saw that Esther was dressed in a blue suit. She had short, dark brown hair that had started to go grey, and she was holding flowers and a rosary. The body had been embalmed, but the flowers had developed a mould that had crept onto her hands and face.

First, Harmon cut clumps of hair as close to the scalp as possible and placed them in plastic bags. He pulled out more hair by the root from the back of her head and the left and right temples. The strands measured a little over 4.5 inches (12 centimetres). He used a razor to take samples of leg and pubic hair, and forceps to pull out the toe- and fingernails. He took samples of fluid from the chest cavity. A microscopic examination of nerve tissues taken from Esther's body showed that the degeneration was similar to what he would expect to find from chronic alcoholism or lead or arsenic poisoning.

Harmon had an advantage over Dr Frank Anderson, the trainee pathologist who performed Esther's first post-mortem, in pinpointing the cause of death. Thanks to Beaton's initial tests at the city analyst lab, Harmon was quite sure that he was looking at arsenic poisoning. He took additional samples of vital organs and paid particular attention to Esther's nails and hair. Because human hair grows at an average rate of about 0.5 inch (1.25 centimetres) a month, and because arsenic

The former Vancouver police headquarters and the old coroner's court and morgue, now the Vancouver Police Museum and Archives on East Cordova Street, in 1956. (Vancouver Archives #447-63)

initially lodges in the root cells of the hair and then remains in that section of hair as it grows out, analysts would be able to estimate both the concentration and rate of consumption of arsenic found in Esther's system.

Harmon placed each specimen in a jar, made sure that they were tightly sealed, and printed the contents clearly on the labels. The cavity fluid was put in a clean bottle. There would be no chance of later being accused of mismatching samples if it should come down to a trial.

The outside of the casket was in good condition, but Harmon wanted to be sure. He scraped dirt from inside and outside the casket and gave these to Eldon Rideout, who would also test the embalming fluid from Simmons & McBride, the undertakers, for arsenic to rule out any possibility of contamination.

At the city analyst's lab, Rideout opened the spoils from the police investigation—a cardboard box filled with exhibits seized from the Castellant home. Inside, he found twenty-nine items, including prescription drugs, wine, Coppertone suntan lotion, garlic salt, hairspray, and a can of weed killer labelled Ortho Triox that contained sodium arsenite, a caustic solution and one of the most toxic forms of arsenic. The label on the can of Ortho gave the arsenic concentration as 5.4 pounds per gallon (0.65 kilograms per litre), which he checked and confirmed. Rideout also noted that there were three ounces (eighty-five grams) missing—more than enough to cause death if given over a period of six or seven months. Rideout found that the Ortho Triox dissolved easily in milk, and he even went as far as to mix a little of the poison in some water, swish it around in his mouth, and spit it out. It had no taste at all.

Rideout would spend the next three months doing more than 300 tests on tissue, bone, and hair samples from Esther's body. He started by retesting Beaton's findings using the Gutzeit test and then developed another, more sensitive method of analysis to test the results again. As expected, the tests revealed massive quantities of arsenic. He found up to 1,500 times more arsenic than would normally be in a human liver, and more than 800 times the amount of arsenic that he would expect to find in a heart.

If arsenic is ingested, it immediately goes to the hair, so Rideout started by cutting several hairs each into twelve sections, measuring one centimetre per section. He found that the roots of the hair contained 353 parts per million of arsenic, decreasing to 9 parts per million at the tip. He also compared the samples of Jeannine's hair that the detectives had taken from the house, and these showed that her hair had a miniscule amount of arsenic—slightly over 1 part per million, exactly what you would expect to find in a healthy human being. If somehow Esther had been accidentally poisoned, then her daughter probably would have also shown some symptoms.

Rideout found that the highest concentration of arsenic was near Esther's scalp. This meant that she had received the largest doses recently, while she was in the hospital. Since she'd been unable to feed herself, it ruled out the possibility of suicide. Someone had to have given it to her.

Although Rideout's tests had provided a rough time frame for the poisoning, coroner Glen McDonald told city analyst Ted Fennell that they had to be a hundred percent certain of their findings. Before he convened an inquest into Esther's death, he wanted a better idea of the amount of arsenic that Esther had unknowingly ingested and when she had ingested it. Fennell contacted the Ontario Attorney General's Crime Detection Laboratory in Toronto (now the Ontario Centre of Forensic Sciences) and asked for their assistance.

A biologist named Norman Erickson at the Toronto lab was involved in groundbreaking hair analysis techniques using a new technology called neutron activation analysis (NAA), which was much more sensitive in detecting arsenic than the tests that Rideout had available to him at the city analyst's lab. Rideout selected samples of hair, including the roots, along with samples of nails and skin and sent them by registered mail to the Toronto lab. "At that time, the only analytical technique that was sufficiently sensitive to analyze for arsenic in small sections of hair or fingernails was neutron activation analysis," says Douglas Lucas, retired director of the Ontario Centre of Forensic Sciences. "We were one of the few labs in North America that could make those analyses using the reactor at McMaster University in Hamilton."

As Lucas explains, when NAA technology was used, hair samples were irradiated in a nuclear reactor to make the arsenic radioactive. The arsenic was then detected and identified with a gamma spectrometer, the results of which gave the ability to estimate the date of ingestion. It was the first time in Canada that neutron activation analysis was used to track the ingestion of poison in a murder case.[18]

---

18 In 1968, the Centre of Forensic Sciences used a similar technique to search for arsenic in the death of Arctic explorer Charles Francis Hall, who died aboard his ship off the northwest coast of Greenland in 1871. The tests were positive for arsenic and it was thought that the murderer used coffee as a delivery system for the poison.

By pulling out hairs longer than 4.5 inches (12 centimetres) and analyzing the arsenic content in each centimeter and then each half centimeter from root to tip, the analysts were able to plot the concentration of arsenic in the hair each month on a chart dating from August 1964 to Esther's death the following July.

The charts showed that Esther had been receiving a steady supply of arsenic, which corresponded to her acute bouts of gastroenteritis and her subsequent recoveries. Most significantly, the tests found that she had been receiving increasing amounts in February and March, and she had received a massive dose within the last thirty to thirty-five days of her life—the period when she was in hospital. It explained the entire clinical picture that Dr Moscovitch had found and confirmed his suspicions that the cause of death was arsenic poisoning.

Reid and McKay now faced the mammoth task of interviewing all twenty-one of the nursing staff who were involved in Esther's care during the seven weeks of her hospital stay. Although several of the nurses commented that the Castellanis seemed like a happy couple, the most helpful comments came from nurses Evelyn Jackson and Gemmel Holtz, and nurse's aide Audrey Hill.

Jackson said she had seen Rene with a milkshake on at least one occasion toward the end of June but didn't notice the empty milkshake containers in the room after Rene left. Holtz mentioned that she had seen Rene bring in cans of 7 Up and milkshakes, but no one could confirm that Esther drank these, that they were even meant for her, or if they were, if they contained anything other than milk, ice cream, or pop.

The detectives perked up when Audrey Hill told them that Rene had given her a ride to her Kitsilano home one night after her shift. "Esther's mother offered to drive me home, as it was around eleven p.m. and I was going off shift. I didn't want her to wait, as I didn't get off until 11:30, so Esther suggested that Rene, her husband, drive me home," she told detectives. Rene was driving the CKNW truck. She thought it was strange when he asked her how much longer Esther had to live. Hill told him she didn't know what was wrong with his wife.

"He said he had ordered an electric stove and an automatic washer and dryer, but he had not picked them up. As he said, 'Why should I if I don't know if she'll ever be out of the hospital, or if she is going to die?'" said Hill. He told her that he would sit in the hospital room and watch, as she had trouble breathing. "She'd gasp every now and then, and the doctors had told him her muscles were deteriorating," she said. "He put two and two together, he said. 'It might be a bad way to look at things, but I have to look to the future. I have my little girl to think of,' and he said that if [his wife] died, he would get a small suite for himself and his little girl, rather than the big house he had."

Mrs Defries, the nursing supervisor, told detectives that one night, after Esther had been put on the seriously ill list, Rene had phoned to ask about his wife's condition. When she told him there was no change, he said, "It's hopeless."

The detectives had to confirm that Esther had been murdered and then identify the murderer. Murder by arsenic poisoning requires a special kind of determination and ruthlessness, thought the detectives. Only someone close to the victim could carry it out, and it seemed particularly diabolical to the detectives that Esther was being poisoned in the hospital, a supposedly safe place where she was being tested and treated for an unknown illness. Rene remained suspect number one. Reid and McKay knew that when a wife is murdered, nine times out of ten, it's the husband who did it, and he is therefore always the first suspect until detectives determine otherwise.

What they couldn't understand was why he didn't have her body cremated. The Roman Catholic Church had allowed cremation since 1963, as long as the ashes weren't scattered. Reid and McKay thought that perhaps Rene had become arrogant and overconfident, and this was also the reason he had not bothered to get rid of the distinctive red-and-yellow striped can of Ortho Triox that they'd found under the kitchen sink. But although the detectives were sure that they had found the source of Esther's problems, they still needed to nail down the delivery system.

"If one were to try to use arsenic for this purpose today, a milkshake sounds like not a bad way to administer it," says Douglas Lucas, formerly of the Ontario Centre of Forensic Sciences. "As soon as Castellani saw the physical form of the arsenic he used, a milkshake would have been an obvious potential delivery system, particularly if his wife had previously shown a fondness for them." And she had. Esther loved vanilla milkshakes, and by the end of her stay in hospital, one of the few things she could still digest was milk.

Rene, they now knew, had the means, the opportunity, and the motive. They had found the Ortho Triox under his kitchen sink, he shared a house with Esther, and he had a younger mistress whom he told people he was going to marry.

Whoever had poisoned Esther must have had some knowledge of the effects of poison on the body. Too much poison would have killed her too quickly, while just enough would eventually kill her while mimicking natural causes. The fact that Rene had experience in metals and poisons from his time at the Trail smelter made him an even more viable suspect in the eyes of the detectives.

There was no insurance policy on Esther, so no monetary gain for Rene from his wife's death. But it was starting to look like this man let little stand in the way of what he wanted, and Esther was the obstacle that had stopped him from having Lolly.

The VPD Homicide Squad in 1967. Bill Porteous is second from the right in the first row, Alex Reid is on the left in the top row, and Archie McKay is second from the left in the top row. (Courtesy Mike Porteous)

CHAPTER 16

THE INQUEST

On October 8, 1965, CKNW boss Bill Hughes asked for and received a letter of resignation from Rene. At the end of the month, Rene and Jeannine moved into the small bungalow Lolly had bought on Argyle Street in East Vancouver. Bud Foxgord, now divorced from Gloria, took their three daughters and moved to California. Rene made sure Jeannine had no contact with her grandparents, aunts, or uncles.

While waiting for the inquest to start on December 1, Rene helped Lolly's stepfather put an addition onto the little house. There were only two bedrooms, so Rene and Lolly slept on the pullout in the living room, and Jeannine and Don each had their own room.

The inquest was held at the coroner's building—and the press were out in full force. Except for a few articles that came out when police announced that arsenic poisoning was the cause of Esther's death, there had been little written about the murder, and headline writers were sharpening their pencils.

The first time that Esther's family saw Rene since the night of her funeral, they were shocked to see him with Lolly, who was wearing the fur coat that Gloria had bought for Esther. "What struck me as funny was, why did he sit at the back of the courtroom on the other side with Lolly Miller? Who the hell was Lolly Miller?" Gloria told author Susan McNicoll in 2006. And did Lolly know that her lover had given her his dead wife's coat?

Gloria was also surprised to see that Rene had brought Albert Mackoff. "He brought his lawyer with him, and the three of them sat by themselves at the back. Why would you come with a lawyer? None of us came with a lawyer. We came to find out how she had died."

She would soon find out.

Judge McDonald told the jury of six—three men and three women—that it was not their job to find out who was responsible but to determine if death was by accident, natural causes, suicide, or murder. He told them that because poison was "such an insidious and innocuous method," a certain amount of hearsay evidence must be allowed to go into the record at the coroner's inquest, but it was not necessarily the truth and for that reason would not be allowed into an actual trial.

Addressing the jury, McDonald noted that it was ironic that a hundred years ago, anyone buying a poison such as arsenic was required to sign for it. But now, sales of arsenic were no longer monitored, and poisons like Ortho Triox could be purchased easily at most hardware stores.

Twenty-seven people were questioned over the three days of the inquest, including Esther's friends and family, Rene's colleagues from CKNW, and hospital medical staff. As was his right, Rene refused to testify.

McDonald questioned Esther's doctors and specialists about the events leading up to her death. He put the Vancouver General Hospital under scrutiny, asking Dr Lawrence Ranta, head of medical services, how it was that Esther could have received arsenic when she was bedridden for several weeks, in their care, and unable to feed herself. Ranta replied that arsenic could not be accidentally fed from supplies in the hospital pharmacy or from any other source within the hospital. "Any arsenic that would be available in the hospital would be under rigid control, and as far as I am aware, arsenic is not available within the hospital as a poisonous substance that is used for the control of pests of any kind," he said. Ranta added that the hospital had no regulations against visitors bringing in food to patients unless the patient was on a special diet. Warren Peterson, the builder and owner of the Hoy Street house that Rene and Lolly had tried to buy just twelve days before Esther's death, the real estate agent who filed their mortgage application, and the banker who interviewed them all testified that Rene and Lolly talked of their marriage plans and agreed to have the mortgage put in their soon-to-be married names.

Although all this information was building a solid foundation for a future trial and filling the newspapers, it was Lolly Miller, the twenty-six-year-old former radio receptionist and Rene's lover, who was the star attraction. It was also the only time that Lolly would have to testify.

Asked about the testimony from Peterson, she said that he was clearly mistaken. "At no time was the subject of marriage brought up." Gillis, the real estate agent, had also misunderstood, she said. He had also been told that she was buying the house in her name, with Rene as the co-signer. "He [Gillis] looked at me and he said, 'Are you getting married?' I said, 'In the future.'" She said that she had no marriage prospects at the time. "I did not realize he thought I was going to be married to Castellani," she said. "And then he said, 'Well, it is not likely that you will get the house,' because I wasn't working at the time." Lolly said that when she and Rene went to the bank to arrange the mortgage, they were both shocked to find that Gillis had made out the application in the names of Adelaide and Rene Castellani.

When McDonald asked Lolly why, after they realized the bank had mistakenly put the application in their joint names, they had allowed it to go through. "I believe Rene did it because he knew how anxious I was to get the house, and I was quite disappointed when [the loans officer] said this, that we would have to produce a certificate of marriage, so we let it go."

Rene had not come down from the BowMac promotion to see her, she said, but she and Don had dropped by the car lot to take him the pyjamas and nightcap that he had asked her mother to make for him. She knew Esther was in the hospital but did not know whether Rene had told her he was co-signing on Lolly's house. "I didn't question Rene about his wife because she was in the hospital, and I didn't want to say anything in case I might upset him."

McDonald said, "I suppose it is candid and proper to ask you, what are your feelings in connection with Mr Castellani now? Has matrimony ever been discussed by you?"

"Yes, now it has," answered Lolly. The romance, though, did not start until they had returned from Disneyland four months before. Rene and his daughter had moved into her house, she told him, and in return for room and board, Rene had built an addition onto the house.

A juror asked, "What was your reaction when you heard perhaps Esther Castellani had died of poison?"

"I was shocked," answered Lolly.

At the end of the third day of the inquest, the jury ruled that the cause of Esther's death was homicide by arsenic poisoning by person or persons unknown. They also recommended that pesticides and herbicides should be sold only after the purchaser's name was recorded in a register maintained by the store.

Shortly after the verdict, detectives Reid and McKay spoke to Rene as he sat in court with Lolly. He turned to them and said, "If you want your washer fixed anytime, call me." As he walked out of the courtroom, he told a photographer, "Not again," while Lolly held up her purse to hide her face. They brushed past photographers on the stairs leading from the court to the street.

As they walked outside, Rene put his arm around Lolly's waist. A few minutes later, several of Esther's relatives came out of the courtroom openly crying.

CHAPTER 17

ARRESTED

Jeannine quickly adapted to living with her new mother and little brother; she didn't have a choice. She was still not allowed to have any contact with her maternal grandparents, aunts, or uncles and their families. "He told me, 'If you talk to them, they'll try and turn you against me, and you'll never see me again and then we can't be a family," says Jeannine. "And that frightened me. I had just lost my mum. I didn't want to lose my dad."

Esther's furniture was brought to Lolly's house. "My mum's wedding dress was in the cedar chest, we had our couch and my bed. He built me a really nice closet in my bedroom. He built an addition on the back of the house. He was always doing something. We just lived as a family. There were kids in the neighbourhood. It was actually quite normal."

Except that Esther was never mentioned. "We never spoke a word about Mum after she was gone, and I just knew not to ask," says Jeannine. "Nobody told me why. The subject was just never brought up. I don't ever remember seeing a newspaper—everything was hidden, hidden, hidden."

On March 31, 1966—five days after 2,000 marchers protesting the Vietnam War held up traffic along Broadway on their trek to the Vancouver courthouse—Rene, a forty-year-old contractor and widower, and Lolly, a twenty-six-year-old widow and homemaker, both of 6331 Argyle Street, applied for a marriage licence that would take effect April 4.

The detectives had put off arresting Rene for as long as possible because they wanted him to think that he had gotten away with murder.

Vietnam War protestors outside the old Vancouver courthouse on West Georgia Street. (Courtesy Bob Cain)

That would make him arrogant and sloppy and, they hoped, lead them to evidence that would strengthen their case and get a conviction.

The marriage licence changed everything. A wife couldn't be forced to testify against her husband—so they arrested Rene before he and Lolly had a chance to marry.

George Garrett, CKNW radio reporter, got the heads up that the detectives would be arresting Rene. "I knew the detectives quite well. They were great guys," says Garrett. "I knew they were investigating, of course, and they had the results of the autopsy and all the rest of it. They said, 'George, we're giving Rene the blue piece of paper today.' That meant they were going to arrest him."

Detectives Reid and McKay obtained an arrest warrant on April 6

Vancouver Court

EXHIBIT D

Rene Castellani

Capital Murder

Date *Application 0595*

N? 58057 D

THE GOVERNMENT OF
THE PROVINCE OF BRITISH COLUMBIA

Marriage Licence

Application for a marriage licence having been duly made to the undersigned on the

31st day of March , 19 66 , in the manner prescribed
by the Marriage Act, and payment of the prescribed licence fee of $5 having been made, in respect
of an intended marriage between the following parties:—

INTENDED BRIDEGROOM

Full name RENE EMILE CASTELLANI

Address 6331 Argyle Street   Vancouver, B. C.

Age 40   Marital status Widower
                                        (Bachelor, widower, or divorcé.)

INTENDED BRIDE

Full name ADELAIDE ANNE MILLER

Address 6331 Argyle Street   Vancouver, B. C.

Age 26   Marital status Widow
                                        (Spinster, widow, or divorcée.)

and all other requirements of the said Act in that behalf having been duly complied with.

This Licence is issued to the said parties, hereby authorizing the solemnization of the said
intended marriage in the Province of British Columbia, pursuant to the Marriage Act, at any time
within three months from the effective date of this Licence, by a minister or clergyman duly registered
under the said Act as authorized to solemnize marriage.

Date effective: The 4th day of April , 19 66

Issued at VANCOUVER , in the Province of British Columbia.

Issuer of Marriage Licences.

MARRIAGE ACT

N? 58057 D

This is your receipt for the Marriage Licence fee. The Marriage
Licence may be obtained from the Issuer of Marriage Licences
upon the presentation of this receipt on
or within three months following this date, provided that all
other requirements of the *Marriage Act* have been met.

Rene and Lolly's marriage licence, March 31, 1966. (Courtesy Susan McNicoll)

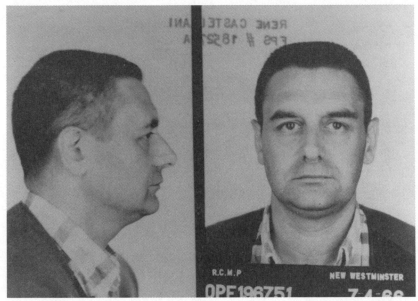

Rene Castellani. (Photograph copyright © Government of Canada. Reproduced with the permission of Library and Archives Canada [2018]. Source: Library and Archives Canada/RG13-B-1, file no. cc 953)

and, along with Staff Sergeant Bill Porteous, went to the house on Argyle Street and arrested Rene just before midnight and charged him with the capital murder of his wife, which meant he would also be eligible for the death penalty.

"I knew something was wrong when I got up in the morning and I could see that Lolly had been crying," says Jeannine. "I said, 'Where is my dad?' And then she told me that he had been arrested." Later that day, he phoned Jeannine from the jail. "He said to me, 'I'm going to get out of here, and we're going to be a family,'" she says. "He never said he didn't do it."

Jeannine was allowed to finish her grade seven year at Little Flower Academy, probably because her grandparents had paid the fees. Before Rene went to jail, he would often drive her to school. After his arrest, she took the bus.

Shortly after the arrest, police paid a visit to Esther's sister, Gloria, who had remarried and was living with her new husband at her parents' house in Kitsilano. In an interview with author Susan McNicoll in 2006, Gloria said that after Rene was arrested, the police followed her for quite a long time, questioned her, and eventually called her into prosecutor Samuel M. Toy's office. Toy asked her about her relationship with her brother-in-law. "I said he was my sister's husband, and I knew him for a number of years," said Gloria. He told her that Rene had said that they'd had an affair, and that she'd murdered Esther out of jealousy.

"Well, I didn't have an affair with him. I never had an affair with Rene. I didn't even like him," said Gloria in the taped interview. "I said there was no way in hell I did. He tried to make it out that I did and I was jealous of my sister. He tried to make out I was a drinker and all of those things. He threw everything at it. I said, yes I do have the odd rum and coke and sometimes, I admit it, I've blacked out and different things happened to me, but I wasn't really a drinker."

By the time Rene's preliminary hearing was held in July 1966 to determine whether there was enough evidence to commit him for trial, he had been in custody for more than three months. Albert Mackoff had successfully argued to have Rene's bail lowered from $25,000 to $15,000, but Rene was unable to raise or borrow the money, so he stayed in jail.

Magistrate James Bartman heard from all the parties who had testified at the inquest several months earlier, including Dr Moscovitch, who told him that Esther had deteriorated in the last seven weeks of her life from a "plump, jovial, pleasant woman to a person gravely ill and almost totally paralyzed." Her condition had improved during her first two weeks in hospital, then steadily deteriorated, he said. When Bartman asked why she had not been tested for arsenic poisoning before her death, Moscovitch said, "The possibility was not considered. It is such a rare occurrence."

Rene's lawyer argued that the prosecution had tried to paint Rene "as a diabolically clever poisoner" who was having an affair, but all the evidence was circumstantial. The judge agreed with prosecutor Stewart McMorran, who argued that Rene was a liar, and that he'd had both motive and opportunity to murder his wife. A trial was scheduled for the following November.

Mike Porteous, current Superintendent of the VPD's Investigation Division, says it is never ideal from the Crown's position to try a case based only on circumstantial evidence, but if they have to, they will. "We like to say the constellation of circumstances leads to a conclusion beyond a reasonable doubt," he says. "So we don't always need to have direct evidence linking the accused to the crime."

Porteous's uncle Bill, now deceased, was in charge of the Castellani investigation in 1965, and he became quite a legend in the police department and in his own family. "It was a fantastic case and a fantastic piece of police work for the day," says his nephew.

If Mike Porteous were investigating the Castellani case today, he would be working with much more sophisticated forensic science, video footage, a team of at least forty personnel, and Crown involvement. "In a big case like Esther Castellani's, you'd form a large team—a video surveillance team, a forensic interview team, a forensic identification team. The detectives would touch none of the exhibits," Porteous says. "All that would be done by specialists. It would cost several hundreds of thousands of dollars." But even so, the case would still have relied on a lot of traditional police work, he says

DNA, for example, which became a staple of police work in the 1990s, and a game changer for solving criminal cases, is of little use in a murder where a husband and wife share the same home and the spouse is a suspect. It may have helped on the can of Ortho Triox, says Porteous. Although Rene denied ever seeing it, and his fingerprints weren't found on the can, if he'd touched the can, it's likely his DNA would have shown up there.

I asked Porteous why Rene risked keeping the can of Ortho Triox in the house—why didn't he just dump it sometime in the three weeks after Esther's death and before the start of the police investigation?

"To me, it isn't that odd," Porteous said. "How would he know that the arsenic would ever show up? There were no *CSI* shows on television," he says. "He's not a sophisticated criminal. This guy, in the criminal world, is kind of a putz. He might be a smart guy, but he's probably going to be relatively uneducated in criminal techniques." It's also possible that he was establishing a reason for Esther's death—that she was using the Triox to kill the weeds in the garden—if arsenic was detected later.

Porteous says that, even today, with the great strides that we've made in science and technology, it's unlikely that arsenic would show up at an autopsy. "That's such an unusual, weird sort of thing. Unless you had a reason to look for it, you wouldn't find it."

It's impossible to know what Rene was thinking, but he'd already fooled a general practitioner and several eminent specialists, so perhaps getting through an autopsy may not have seemed an issue for him. After talking to Gloria and Frank Iaci, he might have been more concerned with what the police would think if he didn't authorize an autopsy, so it was worth the risk.

There are two parts to a murder case, says Porteous: "A) finding out who did it, and in the great majority of cases they do find out who did it. The harder part is B) proving the case. Old-fashioned interviews and autopsies don't change that much. We would exhaust our traditional techniques and see if we could prove the case that way, and if we couldn't meet the threshold of proof, we would go to more advanced covert techniques."

Fifty years ago, covert techniques weren't usually part of the investigative tool kit. Bill Porteous and his two detectives would not have had access to video evidence, which could have been a huge help in seeing who had visited Esther in the hospital and brought her food, and when they had helped to feed her. If milkshakes were the delivery system, video would have showed how they were disposed of—a question that took up a lot of time in both of Rene's trials, the preliminary hearing, and the inquest.

"Video would be able to show every time Rene came to the hospital and what he gave her. If he produced a cup from White Spot, they would canvas every White Spot restaurant and get the purchase records. They would be able to track his movements through the video. The other huge one is they would be able to get all of his phone records between him and the mistress and anybody else related to the case. Police could obtain those records—all obtained by warrant or judicial order—and produce them in court. What you are doing is narrowing it down from being a broadly circumstantial case to a circumstantial case supported by independent evidence."

Speaking of the mistress, I asked him if Lolly had ever been a suspect or an accomplice, something I couldn't see evidence of from police investigation interviews and trial transcripts. Did they just not have any evidence linking her to the murder, or did they have a hard time thinking that an attractive young woman could be involved? Although Porteous can't speculate about what they were thinking half a century ago, he says that even today, it's easier to interview a person as a witness rather than a suspect, where they would now be subject to all of the rights and protections under the 1982 Canadian

Charter of Rights and Freedoms. Even so, Porteous says that if he were investigating this case today, he would treat Lolly as a suspect.

"One of the things that you do in these kinds of cases is always look for a 'divide and conquer,'" he says. "Is there more than one person who knows about this murder, and who is the weak link? Who is at risk for aiding or abetting or conspiring or being an accessory after the fact, which we can then leverage and turn them into a witness for the Crown? I would try and put her in a position of extreme risk from the justice system should she continue to support this guy who is a murderer, whom I would portray as a Lothario and unfaithful—and [I would imply that she] would be his next victim."

Porteous also referred to a theory known as Occam's (or Ockham's) razor, which states "that when presented with a whole set of options, the most obvious solution is almost always the right solution. If I get a murdered wife, my first suspect is the husband, almost always. Right off the bat, that's most likely statistically."

A slow poisoning, such as Esther Castellani's, would also indicate that it was a family member, he says. "A stranger would use an act of violence—stabbing, shooting, or strangling. Even if it's premeditated, an assassination," he says. "Why would you poison somebody you don't know? It would have to be planned, and if it's planned, it leads to either an enemy or goes back to motive, and especially with a female victim, you always go back to the family."

According to Porteous, the other two things the police have to prove are motive and the details of the act of murder itself. "He's having an affair, so he's got a motive, and he's the husband, so he would come under the lens completely," he says. "Even before we interviewed him, we would have intensive surveillance on him and find out what he did when he was first contacted by the police. Did he try and destroy evidence? Did he try and cover up his tracks?"

The fact that Rene initially lied to police about his affair with Lolly would also be useful later in court. "Guilty people deny things," Porteous says. "The jury would wonder why an innocent man would deny that he was having an affair."

In the sequence of interviews with relatives, friends, and persons of interest, detectives interviewed Rene first and then went to Esther's close friend, Margie Scott. When they found out about the affair and who Rene's mistress was, they would have obtained a production order that compelled the bank to hand over any documents pertaining to Lolly and Rene's financial affairs. The detectives quickly learned about their joint application for a mortgage, the name of Lolly's previous landlord, and Rene's precarious financial position.

"You want to snare them into that web of deceit—'I never visited the hospital that day,' 'I never bought that milkshake,' 'I never was going to go away on holiday,' 'I don't have a mistress,' or 'I didn't take a mortgage out with her,'" Porteous says. "If you do all of that stuff and put it to them at trial, it's devastating for the accused. Especially if it forces him to get on the stand. If a defence lawyer puts his client on the stand, it's usually a Hail Mary. From what I've seen of people, it's pretty hard to get on the stand under oath and lie through your teeth and have anybody believe you."

In the course of his work, Mike Porteous is no stranger to psychopaths. "When people hear the word 'psychopathy,' they think Charles Manson. But psychopaths are charming and intelligent, they are motivated for self-promotion, they think they are smarter than anyone else, and they tend to have magnetic personalities."

Porteous had just described Rene to a T.

Forensic psychologist Dr Heather Burke says that Rene's lack of emotion and level of callousness also suggest that he had some of the hallmark traits of a psychopath. "Some psychopaths are very charming and charismatic. They are clever, they are entertaining, and they are fun," she says. "Rene was an intelligent guy. He was superficially charming, and he lacked empathy and remorse. He could be pretty manipulative, but he was smart and funny and a natural salesman, and he was able to succeed because of his intelligence."

The trip to Disneyland seems particularly callous but not surprising, says Burke. "I have seen that before with psychopathic offenders," she says. "They are able to do these kinds of things and not skip a beat. They just carry on with life, and they don't seem to realize or care how that looks to other people."

Psychopaths seem quite normal until you get in their way, says Burke.

Jail cell at Oakalla Prison Farm. (Vancouver Archives #1184-2268)

CHAPTER 18
ON TRIAL FOR LIFE

Rene's trial started at 11:20 a.m. on October 31, 1966, accompanied by dramatic newspaper headlines: "Castellani Took Milkshake to Wife, Nurse Testifies"; "Mother in Tears at Murder Trial"; and "Affair Proved, Not Murder Says Castellani's Lawyer."

Rene's lawyer used eleven challenges to get every woman who was a potential juror eliminated to produce an all-male panel. The reasoning was that women would be sympathetic to Esther and convict Rene for his adultery. Albert Mackoff hoped that the all-male panel would take a "boys will be boys" approach and sympathize with a man who had strayed.

The *Vancouver Sun* reported that Rene wore a dark grey suit, blue tie, and white shirt and "answered the charge today with the words 'not guilty' in a low but firm voice" to a packed public gallery at the law courts. Esther's mother, the reporters noted, wore black.

As expected from the preliminary hearing a few months before, the Crown's case was three-pronged, based on means, opportunity, and motive. The prosecution argued that Rene was having an affair with a woman he planned to marry, and that he planned his wife's death and had both the means and the opportunity to kill her. The chief exhibit was a can of Ortho Triox—the weed killer found in the Castellanis' kitchen—and the main evidence centred on the presence of arsenic in the hairs taken from Esther's head.

Dr Moscovitch's evidence was graphic and heart-wrenching. He told the court that when he admitted Esther to hospital, she had sensations of pins and needles and burning in her fingers extending to her forearms, and then in her feet and legs. "This condition became steadily worse during her stay in hospital," he said. The initial symptoms were followed by intense pain, followed by hypersensitivity and then no sensation at all in her extremities. "She had tremendous spasms in her legs," he said. Moscovitch said that shortly before her death in the hospital, she had become a paraplegic with complete paralysis in her upper and lower extremities. "We considered the most likely diagnosis was an acute [viral] infection, affecting several nerves."

Most damning, though, was the timing. Dr Moscovitch said that Esther was "reasonably comfortable" for the first two weeks that she spent in hospital, but at six p.m. on June 13—the day after Rene came down from the BowMac sign promotion, the Crown prosecutor noted—she suffered nausea and vomiting again shortly after eating her evening meal.

The following day, Moscovitch asked if Esther had come in contact with paint fumes, and Rene told him that she had done some painting with a spray gun at Joyce Dayton's earlier that year. It was the first time paint had been mentioned to Moscovitch, though Rene had been suggesting it to colleagues even before Esther first entered hospital in May. Tests for lead poisoning proved negative, and Rene never brought him the sample of paint that Moscovitch had asked for.

Later, when Dr Moscovitch learned that Rene had told a colleague that Esther had almost died in early June, he was also quite surprised. Her condition during that week was not considered serious. "I told the family her condition was difficult to diagnose and that she would likely be in hospital for several months, but she was not put on the seriously ill list until three days before her death."

Other witnesses testified that Rene had told them different stories about what doctors were saying was behind his wife's illness and were surprised to hear conflicting stories. Over coffee in May, shortly after Esther was admitted to hospital, Rene told Donald Jackson, a New

Westminster printer, that Esther had got poison into her system after spraying in the garden, and "it was just a matter of time."

In early June, Rene had told CKNW's Erm Fiorillo that they had nearly "lost" her, and he told Mel Cooper that it could be lead poisoning from when Esther was painting Joyce Dayton's store. Gina Steeves, a secretary at CKNW, said she asked after Esther daily. "On one occasion, he said the doctors maintained she had toxic poisoning brought on by spray painting or weed killer which she had been using."

Rene embellished a bit further when talking to Mauri Hesketh, telling the news editor that it might have something to do with a type of insecticide that his wife used on the garden. An avid gardener, Hesketh told him that common pesticides could be very dangerous, and if he suspected insecticide was the cause, he should tell the attending doctor. Rene's story changed again when he told Wally Garrett that his neighbours were enthusiastic gardeners and it was possible they had used some kind of toxic spray that affected Esther.

As they had at the preliminary hearing, two nurses from VGH testified that they had seen Rene bring milkshakes into the hospital, though they didn't know whether he or Esther had drunk them or what happened to the containers afterward. Audrey Hill testified, as she had at the inquest, that Rene had casually asked when she thought Esther would die—a question she found bizarre coming from the dying woman's husband.

Dr James Rigsby Foulkes, head of the Department of Pharmacology at UBC, said that he had examined the test results, and it was quite clear that Esther had consumed substantial amounts of arsenic. Foulkes said Esther's arsenic intake fell into three periods: a long period of several months, a short period of two months during which the dose was increased, and finally a large increase that began about five weeks before her death.

This was a potential challenge for the prosecution. Five weeks before her death, Rene was up on the BowMac sign, and much of their case argued that she had not received arsenic during that nine-day period (between June 4 and 12) but that her intake spiked again June 13, the day after Rene came down from the tower.

Even the results and charts that came from the sensitive neutron activation analysis tests, which included rate of hair and nail growth on a woman of Esther's height and weight, couldn't be exact. Put on the stand, the best any analyst could say was that the amount of arsenic and the time period when it was ingested were based on an interpretation of the results. The prosecution's case became stronger when they could chart the days that Esther became ill and matched them to the Toronto lab's estimates of when the arsenic was ingested, based on samples taken from her hair and nails.

If there was any possibility in the minds of the jury that Esther had received arsenic while Rene was on top of the BowMac sign, then they had to try to prove or at least suggest that he had come down from the sign during the night and given Esther the arsenic. Before the promotion, he had told Joyce Dayton that he planned to come down from the sign in the early hours of the morning to visit his wife. He told Mauri Hesketh that he could come down in the early hours of the morning if no one was around, and he told Gerry Davies that he wanted to skip one of the cut-ins so he could visit his wife. Prosecutor Samuel Toy hammered that point home.

The problem for the prosecution was that nobody had seen Rene climb down from the sign or leave the well-lit car park—not the night guard, not any of the nurses that sat at the station outside Esther's room, and certainly not Esther. Or, if she had, she mentioned it to no one. And although Toy proved theoretically that Rene could have entered the hospital unseen through a back door at any time of the night, so could anyone else who knew it was kept open.

The prosecution decided to rely on another expert witness—Dr Harold Taylor, who headed up the pathology lab at VGH and was department head of pathology at UBC. Taylor testified that if Esther had not ingested arsenic between June 4 and June 12, the concentrations in the charts from the Ontario Centre of Forensic Sciences would still fit. The human body is not like a clock, he told the jury. "I couldn't tell you on what date or on what dates the arsenic in the first centimeter was ingested, and I refuse to pinpoint an exact date." It could have been ingested anywhere in the last thirty to thirty-five days of her life, or it could have been administered on the day before her death, he said.

The evidence that appeared to impress the jury was Sheila Luond's testimony about how she had visited Esther about a week before she died and found Rene trying to force feed her, and then he'd demanded that Sheila throw the uneaten portion down the toilet.

Until the trial, Esther and Rene's friends, colleagues, and family had clung to the hope that Rene had not murdered his wife. But as the trial went on and the evidence built, there was no one except Jeannine, Rene's sister Jeanne, and perhaps Lolly who clung to his innocence.

Gloria (Iaci) Cameron, Frank Iaci's cousin, was a good friend to both Esther and Rene and suffered through the trial. She says, "I didn't attend Rene's trial, but I remember how stunned everyone here was. It was so hard for Frank because, at the beginning, he wanted to believe that Rene was innocent, but as time went on, he knew he wasn't. Frank said, 'I believe he did it.' And he did say that at the trial, and I think that was so difficult for him."

During cross-examination, Rene's lawyers tried to make Frank Iaci look like a terrible Crown witness with two failed marriages that both ended after his wives divorced him for adultery and cruelty (the only grounds available for divorce before 1968). He said that he'd met Rene when they were both still single, and he'd became close friends with Rene and later Esther. Jeannine called him Uncle Frank, he said, and he was very fond of her but admitted that he had not seen her since the day after Esther's funeral. He explained that this was only because he couldn't get near her after Rene took her away to live with Lolly.

George Garrett reported on the trial for CKNW. "I just reported it as fairly as possible," he says. "I think CKNW was really worried about the fallout. It's about the worst public relations you can get. But I think it's overpowered by the fact that we were well accepted in the community. We were known for fair coverage, and I think people appreciated that we covered it just the way that we covered any other story." Although few people following the trial would have been unaware that Rene was a former CKNW staffer, the station was trying to distance itself as much as possible. Any mention in their news reports described Rene as a "radio promotion manager," or similar generic term.

"It was a big shock to think that somebody that you worked with could be capable of this," says Norm Grohmann. "I guess there was some buzz at coffee break along the lines of 'Do you think he did it?' You get people who are not in favour of anyone cheating on their wife because it went against their code of ethics, so hang the bastard. And CKNW management, although they were very publicity conscious, this wasn't the publicity they needed, that somebody who worked there could actually murder somebody. I don't think management could have been too happy with the notoriety. Not all publicity is good publicity."

In the end, the jury heard from forty-six Crown witnesses. Albert Mackoff told the jury that the Crown had "nothing but suspicion and guesses" on which to base the murder charge. Rene did not testify, and Mackoff offered no defence but managed to score a few points on key Crown evidence.

Detective Reid admitted that the only identifiable fingerprints found on the can of Triox were from Detective McKay. Two other smudges on the can couldn't be identified.

Assistant city analyst Eldon Rideout could not swear that the arsenic found in Esther's body came from that can of Triox or prove that Rene had given it to her, he told Mackoff, only that the weed killer was found under Rene's kitchen sink and the missing amount was roughly the same dosage needed to kill her.

Prosecutor Toy argued that Rene wasn't all that clever; he'd had no idea that hair samples could show the deposit of arsenic and the time at which it was deposited. "Was it just pure coincidence that the day after Rene came down from the tower her generally improved condition reversed itself, the vomiting started again, the blood started again, everything went haywire, and her deterioration was on a straight run downhill from then on?" he asked the jury.

Mackoff told Justice Ruttan and the jury that motive and opportunity were not proof of guilt. And although that may be true, it held little sway with the jury. They were given a choice of guilty of capital murder or acquittal. In less than five hours, they came back with a guilty verdict and in just over five minutes decided not to recommend clemency. The judge had no choice but to impose the death penalty.

Sitting in the prisoner's box with his arms folded, Rene watched the jurors file back into the courtroom. He flicked a glance toward the ceiling at the world "guilty," then looked straight ahead. Sheila Luond let out a shuddering sob, and Gloria wept uncontrollably.

Asked if he had anything to say, Rene remained as emotionless as he had throughout the nine-day trial. He stood and said quietly, "I have nothing to say."

"The sentence of this court is that you be taken to the prison whence you came and remain there until Tuesday the 21st of February

1967, when you shall be taken to the place of execution and hanged by the neck until you are dead," the judge said. "May the Lord have mercy on your soul."

A crowd of about thirty spectators, some of whom had attended the trial every day, remained silent throughout the proceedings. A few waited in the chilly night air outside the Hornby Street exit from the courthouse to watch Rene, handcuffed and holding a lit cigarette, be driven back to jail in a marked RCMP car.

Mackoff, visibly shaken by the verdict, said they would appeal.

Two weeks after Rene was returned to Oakalla Prison Farm, the Department of Justice asked the institution's medical officer to assess his physical and mental condition. The doctor noted: "Good general health and has been a 'model' prisoner throughout and a stabilizing influence on others. He is a highly intelligent man, most competent and courageous. No area of fallibility has been evident, any emotion is deeply concealed."

Now Rene's life was literally in the hands of his lawyer. He would spend Christmas 1966 wondering what would come first—the date for a retrial or his execution.

CHAPTER 19
THE SUMMER OF LOVE

Rene Castellani's appeal was not heard until February 1967. Before five justices of the British Columbia Court of Appeal, Albert Mackoff claimed that Justice Ruttan forgot to explain Rene's defence to the jury until three hours after the jury began its deliberations. He argued that even though Ruttan had realized his mistake and recalled the jury to explain, this served only to belittle the defence in the minds of the jury as a mere afterthought. The time that Ruttan spent dealing with the defence's theory was disproportionate to the time he spent explaining the Crown's side, Mackoff said. Mackoff asked the court to quash the conviction that was based entirely on circumstantial evidence, arguing that Castellani's actions and behaviour were those of an innocent man.

If Rene was a "secret poisoner," as the Crown had attempted to prove, he would not have agreed to call in medical specialists and would never have agreed to an autopsy on his wife's body. He would not have left a can of arsenic-based weed killer in the house. "The Triox was not hidden. It was under the sink," said Mackoff. "Castellani's wife died July 11, and yet the can was not found until August 3. If Castellani was a poisoner, it is unthinkable that he would leave the weapon of his murder sitting openly in his home. He would have got rid of it. He had ample time."

Mackoff emphasized to the appeal justices that Rene's fingerprints had not been found on the can, though his wife had been poisoned over a period of at least five months.

Yes, he'd lied about his affair with Lolly Miller, said Mackoff, but so would "ninety-nine percent of married men who are involved in extramarital relationships." And, yes, he told people that he was getting

A couple rock to the electric music of Country Joe and the Fish at Vancouver's first be-in at Ceperley Park, Stanley Park, on Easter Sunday, March 26, 1967. (Photo by Ken Oakes, courtesy *Vancouver Sun*)

a divorce and marrying Lolly, but that was just a matter of Rene seeking to portray "an air of respectability," said Mackoff.

The justices were not swayed by Mackoff's argument that someone else could have poisoned Esther. There was simply no evidence to support this suggestion. Although Rene hadn't succeeded in moving the trial jury, ten days before his execution date, the prisoner was given a reprieve from the gallows. But it wasn't Mackoff's arguments that convinced the judges to allow an appeal, it was trial Justice Ruttan's suggestion to the jury that they could consider Rene the murderer because of his "bad character, deceitfulness, immorality, and general pattern of life." The appeal judges found this to be "highly prejudicial" and awarded Rene a new trial.

I asked George Garrett, who worked with Rene at CKNW and later covered his trial, if he thought that Rene had been convicted, in essence, for his infidelity. Although his adulterous behaviour may have shocked a conservative jury whose values were still locked in the 1950s, outside the courtroom, the '60s were in full swing. "The 1960s were the turning point," Garrett says, "and there was a tilting of values, but in those days, cheating on your wife was really frowned upon."

But on March 26, 1967, Easter Sunday, the newspapers had all but forgotten Rene Castellani and his upcoming appeal trial and were instead focused on the Human Be-In at Stanley Park—a local take on the be-in that had taken place in San Francisco's Golden Gate Park two months before and set the tone for the Summer of Love. Vancouver's event was much smaller, but about a thousand hippies, and three times as many onlookers, turned up at Ceperley Park near Second Beach wearing colourful attire—beaded vests with jeans and tattered evening gowns, even monk and clown costumes. They danced to bands like Country Joe and the Fish, dropped LSD, and carried signs that read, *Make Love, Not War*, and *Burn Pot, Not People*. This event officially marked the beginnings of Vancouver's counterculture and set the stage for the launch of the movement's newspaper, the *Georgia Straight*, the first issue of which hit the streets on May 5, 1967, with a cover price of ten cents.

The *Straight* gave a voice to anti-establishment values, to pot-smoking hippies, and to draft dodgers looking for refuge from American conscription and the Vietnam War. Articles about growing marijuana

Poster advertising upcoming Vancouver concerts for Country Joe and the Fish. (From the collection of Rob Frith, owner of Neptoon Records)

and cartoons that showed naked, stoned anti-heroes incensed Vancouver's stodgy and repressive middle-class culture. The *Straight* was banned on the streets of New Westminster, where CKNW had its offices, and its staff were subjected to police harassment and legal problems, including several obscenity charges.

But although these events were plastered over the newspapers, by September the city was once again talking about the murder of Esther Castellani. Esther's sensational murder, which had already taken up so much space in the newspapers and on radio and television for the previous two years, would continue to earn headlines and be a main topic of conversation at cocktail parties and around office coffee urns. The media attention would also guarantee that Rene's second trial attracted a huge crowd, many of them women.

The substance of Rene's appeal trial was the same as the first. The Crown built its case entirely on circumstantial evidence, arguing that Rene murdered his wife so that he would be free to marry his much younger lover. Rene's new lawyers, Charles Maclean[19] and John Davies, still weren't mounting much of a defence—probably because of a lack of cash from their client—but their trial strategy had changed. They would put their client on the stand to deny that he killed his wife. And they would put Rene's thirteen-year-old daughter, Jeannine, on the stand, prepped and ready to cast reasonable doubt. But not before hammering under cross-examination Gloria Yusep—Esther's attractive and unbalanced younger sister.

It was Gloria's first time testifying in court, and she took the stand on the fifth day of the trial in front of a packed courtroom and a jury made up of nine men and three women.

"Jack Webster came over to me and said, 'There's going to be a bomb dropped this afternoon.' I didn't know the bomb was going to be me," Gloria told Susan McNicoll in 2006.

Under cross-examination by John Davies, Gloria broke down in tears when asked if it was true that she was only Esther's half sister. "I don't know that," she said. Justice Victor Dryer adjourned the court for five minutes while Gloria got herself under control. When Davies repeated his question, Gloria said, "I didn't know the details on that, no. I never discussed it."

Davies asked Gloria about a period in 1964 when she and her sister were not speaking to each other. Gloria said that she was in California for five months, but that her sister did not visit or talk to her on the phone

---

19 Charles Maclean was a teacher before graduating from UBC law school in 1963. He was elected as the BC Conservative candidate for North Vancouver–Capilano in 1968 and became a radio talk show host in the 1990s.

after her return to Vancouver. "She wouldn't talk to me," Gloria told Davies. "I was having trouble with my marriage, and she didn't want to be involved in it."

While she was still married to Bud Foxgord, the father of her three daughters, Gloria had moved to California and married George Ridgeway, "on the advice of Dr Foxgord to do so," she told Davies, so that Foxgord could divorce Gloria for bigamy, in 1964. She said that she had reconnected with her sister the April before her death and had visited about three times after her sister moved into the new duplex.

Gloria agreed with Davies that Esther was a woman of considerable moral standing. "You don't put yourself in that category, do you?" he asked.

"No, I don't," answered Gloria.

In the early 1960s, her then-husband Bud Foxgord, a general practitioner, had her admitted to the Crease Clinic at Riverview mental hospital. Later, she spent time at the Hollywood Sanitarium, a private hospital in New Westminster that treated patients with alcohol and drug addictions. Just before her divorce in 1964, she had attempted suicide for the third time by slashing her wrists. In the spring of 1965, she had taken sleeping pills and was taken to St. Paul's Hospital. She was there at the same time as Esther. "They said I wasn't trying to commit suicide, I was trying to get sympathy," she said on the stand. "They said if I really wanted to, I would jump."

She had married Elmer Yusep a few months after Esther's death and continued to run an art supplies store and gallery called the Canvas Shack in Kerrisdale.

Although the conservative audience was delighted by what they would have considered Gloria's loose morals and unconventional lifestyle, which made for front-page stories the next day, the followers

Gloria and Bud Foxgord in happier days, circa 1950s.

of the Castellani trial were eagerly anticipating the main events—to hear Rene Castellani testify for the first time, and to see his only defence witness, his daughter, Jeannine.

SENTENCED TO DEATH for arsenic murder of his wife, former broadcaster Rene Castellani is led handcuffed from Vancouver courthouse Thursday.

—Dave Buchan Photo

Castellani Sentenced to Die; Defence to File Appeal

Rene Castellani returns to jail in handcuffs after his trial.
(*Vancouver Sun*, November 12, 1966)

CHAPTER 20
CIRCUMSTANTIAL EVIDENCE

Rene and Jeannine, the only two witnesses for the defence, did not testify until near the end of the second week of the trial. Rene walked briskly from the prisoner's box to the witness stand when his name was called. He was then sworn in. Maclean said, "Rene Castellani—look at the jury. Did you murder your wife, Esther?"

"I did not," he answered clearly.

Maclean then handed his client over to prosecutor Toy for cross-examination, and for the first time, people heard Rene talk about his wife, her murder, and his affair.

To try to establish his knowledge of science and poison, Toy questioned him closely about his education. Rene left school after grade ten, he told him, and his first job was at a smelter in Trail, BC. "That was in the acid plant, was it not?" asked Toy. "Yes, in the lead burner section," answered Rene, who also acknowledged that he enjoyed reading, writing, and acting in plays.

In 1960, he told Toy, he became manager of his brother-in-law's company Hydro Pure Sales. Dr Foxgord handled the science, he told Toy, and Rene sold an ultraviolet-ray product designed to be used in conjunction with a swimming pool filter to purify water and eliminate the use of chlorine. "Dr Foxgord and his wife, Gloria, had purchased the company, and it was in a bankrupt state," Rene said. "My time was spent primarily in selling the product so that we could get some money."

Toy painted him as a liar, referring to testimony from Lolly's landlord, the builder and owner of the prospective house, the mortgage broker, and the banker that he was getting a divorce and that he and

Esther Castellani's Sister
Denies Death Threat Charge

LATE FLASHES

$300 Million Contract Signed

Rescuers
Race In
After SOS

Drawing of the court proceedings by *Vancouver Sun* cartoonist Roy Peterson as
Jeannine Castellani took the stand, October 5, 1967.

Lolly were getting married. Toy pointed out that while Rene was telling
Bill Hughes and Erm Fiorillo that he was not having an affair, he had
been seeing Lolly since the summer of 1964. "It was a deliberate lie,
was it not?" asked Toy.

"Yes," answered Rene.

Although Rene lied about his mistress, his divorce, and his
Disneyland holiday with Jeannine, Lolly, and Don, he was telling
the truth at all other times, he said. He had not fed his wife in the
presence of his sister-in-law, and although he encouraged her to eat,
he certainly did not try to feed her against her will. He also said that
several of his former colleagues were mistaken when they testified
that he had mentioned weed killer or insecticide; he had only ever
said that Esther had come in contact with paint.

After three hours on the stand, he was dismissed, and then his
daughter was called to give testimony. Thirteen-year-old Jeannine
came into the courtroom accompanied by Lolly Miller. Rene smiled
at the pair as they entered but did not speak to them.

After Jeannine took the stand and was sworn in as a witness, Justice Dryer asked her a series of questions to make sure she knew the meaning of taking an oath on the Bible. She told him that she had never taken an oath but knew it as "a value taken before God to tell the truth."

Jeannine told the court that she was a grade-nine student at David Thompson Secondary and had lived with Lolly Miller and her son, Don, in East Vancouver for more than two years. It had been nearly two years since she had seen her father, she said.

After a dozen or so introductory questions, Maclean asked her, "What was the relationship between Gloria and your mother?"

"My aunt Gloria was always jealous of my mum, and she threatened to kill her. She would phone up my mum and threaten her," she said.

Gloria, who was sitting in the front row of the spectators' gallery, screamed, "Jeannine!"

Sheriff F. W. Wells called for order. Jeannine didn't look at her aunt but stared straight ahead at the jury, just as she had been told to do by her father's lawyers. Jeannine then told the court that her aunt used to "prowl around the house at night. I saw her in her car—a white Cadillac. I shut off all the lights, and I sat with my mum because she was scared."

Gloria sat on the edge of her chair, tightly gripping the railing that separated the gallery from the court. She stared at Jeannine throughout the remainder of her evidence.

Asked if she had ever seen her aunt Gloria preparing food for her mother, Jeannine said, yes, that she had come the same day her mother went into hospital and made banana-orange and black cherry Jell-O. She said Gloria shut the door to the kitchen and wouldn't let her in. Later, after Gloria had left and the Jell-O had set, her mother ate some and shortly afterward became sick. She said that two detectives questioned her in August 1965, but she hadn't told them about the Jell-O because they had not asked her about it.

Jeannine and Gloria, circa 1960.

Asked about the trip to Disneyland following her mother's funeral, Jeannine said that it was her idea. "We took three days to get there and stayed in motels along the way. My dad and I slept in a bed, and Lolly and Don slept in another bed," she lied.

Jeannine had been well primed for her testimony. As Maclean led her through the questions, she told him that she had seen her mother use weed killer. "One morning, I saw her mixing it, because the dandelions bugged her," she said.

Prosecutor Toy questioned her again about the Jell-O and the timing of her mother's illness, and then asked her if she had spoken to Lolly Miller about what she was going to say in court. Jeannine told him yes. "And you have gone over it with her?" asked Toy. Jeannine said she had. "How many times?" he asked. "We went over it with Mr Maclean, Mr Davies, and Mr Mackoff and Lolly about two or three times," she said.

Jeannine's testimony made the front page of both dailies the next day.

More than half a century after giving evidence, Jeannine has a completely different recollection of those events. She admits that she lied on the stand after being coached by her dad's lawyers. Jeannine now says that her testimony was well rehearsed; they told her what questions to expect and how she should answer.

"You're little, but you know something's not right," Jeannine says. "I wanted to think Dad didn't do it. I was just a kid. When I was in the room talking with my dad's lawyer, he made me believe the things that I was saying. 'Remember, Jeannine, this happened like this, don't you remember this?' And I just went with it, knowing that I wasn't sure that's really what happened, but I just wanted to be with my dad no matter what the cost. I'm not going to say no to these adults, this big huge lawyer that he had. I'm going to do whatever it takes to get my dad out of jail and spend my life with him. I didn't realize how it would affect me later by doing what I did when I was thirteen."

I asked her if she ever remembered her aunt threatening her mother or her mother being scared of Gloria. Jeannine says she doesn't remember her aunt peering through the window, but she does remember turning the lights off one time and her mother being less than enthusiastic at a visit from her sister.

"There were times when Mum didn't want anything to do with her, and I remember my mum getting calls from her and getting upset, but I didn't really know why," she tells me. "Dad had told me that Aunt Gloria had always been jealous of my mum. And I thought, why would she be jealous of my mum? She had nothing compared to what my aunt had. I think it was my mum's character that she was jealous of, because Mum was a true person. There was no fakeness. She was genuine, everybody liked her. I always felt very safe and adored when I was with Mum. She was a very comforting person."

I asked what she knew about Gloria's suicide attempts. "My grandparents always blamed it on her husband, on the doctor—he was always giving her pills—but I think it goes back to their childhood."

She admits that it's possible that Gloria made Jell-O for her mother, and in fact, Gloria admitted that it did happen. But Jeannine says she can't remember being shut out of the kitchen. "I do remember that testimony. I remember feeling kind of weird when I said it because I didn't feel like it was really correct. There was this uneasy feeling, and then when I heard her scream in the courtroom, I thought, what is going on? I was just petrified."

I asked her whether it was true that Lolly and her dad had slept in separate beds on the Disneyland trip. "No, I was told to say that," she admitted.

Another piece of key testimony was the story that she had seen her mother using weed killer. It seemed a strange thing for a child to remember in such detail. "That never happened," she said. "My mum wasn't a gardener. I don't remember that at all."

After Jeannine had finished testifying, Rene's defence lawyers took her to see her father, who was being held in the jail. The day, which had already been emotionally charged, was about to get worse for Jeannine, as she found herself sharing an elevator with her weeping grandmother and aunts. Mabel Luond tried to talk to her granddaughter, but Jeannine broke away from her and began to cry.

Maclean left a hysterical Mabel crying on the other lawyer's shoulder and spirited Jeannine away to another part of the building to see her dad. Rene, who had earlier testified that he had rediscovered God while in Oakalla prison over the past seventeen months, cried as he gave Jeannine his rosary as an RCMP officer stood guard.

"Everything's all right, Dad," the newspaper reported that Jeannine told him. It was the first time they had seen each other since Rene was arrested in April 1966, and the meeting lasted only a couple of minutes.

Adult Jeannine remembers going to see her dad after the trial for a very short time. "I was able to hug him and say goodbye, but I didn't know it was going to be goodbye forever—you're not thinking like that at thirteen. I just knew he was going away. I don't remember how I was after that. If he was crying, I would remember that."

Meanwhile, on recall by prosecutor Toy in the courtroom, Gloria took the witness stand and vehemently denied her young niece's charge that she had threatened to kill Esther. She said she had never gone to their house and peered in the windows. She hadn't been at Esther's the day that she was taken to the hospital; she was at home with her mother. Mabel Luond later corroborated Gloria's story.

Asked about her feelings toward her sister, Gloria replied, "I liked her very much. I have no ill feelings toward her."

In 2006, Gloria told author Susan McNicoll that people had hidden cameras under their coats and were taking pictures of her coming and going from the trial. When McNicoll asked Gloria what she was thinking while she was listening to the evidence, she said, "That he was definitely guilty."

Some of the most incriminating evidence against Rene came from his sister-in-law Sheila Luond. She had testified that she had seen Rene feeding Esther shortly before her death. Esther was clearly in distress, she said, and Rene had finally given up and then bullied Sheila into flushing the uneaten food down the toilet. Although it's unclear why Rene couldn't have just flushed the food himself, after hearing Sheila's testimony, it would have been hard not to think that he had added arsenic to the dish.

In an attempt to take the edge off some of Sheila's testimony, Maclean told the jury that the Crown was asking them to convict on "a tissue of faulty recollection, speculation, suspicion and, in at least one instance, of lies." He told them that her testimony was "the most damning piece of evidence the Crown was able to produce against Rene. It's an absolute black wicked lie, which is designed to hang this man, by somebody who hates him. I say to you now unequivocally, Mrs Sheila Luond is a liar because the records show she is a liar," said Maclean. He drew the jury's attention to two separate hospital records that showed that Esther had received a blood transfusion at the same time Sheila had claimed Rene was trying to feed her. "The witness is so convinced of his guilt that she will go there and say anything."

Maclean then tried to get some sympathy for Rene's affair, at least in the minds of the nine male jurors. "If we're going to hang men for adultery, there aren't enough lampposts in Vancouver to accommodate them," he said. In a murder case, police always look first to the spouse, he said, and this blinded them to other potential suspects.

"They have got the biggest selection of gossip, rumour, and speculative nonsense I've ever heard in a courtroom," he said. "The Crown alleges Castellani's motive was his love for Mrs Miller. I wish people would call her Adelaide," he said, "When they say 'Lolly,' it sounds like a dance hall girl with a feather in her hat. She's an ordinary girl."

Crown prosecutor Toy told the jury that there were two issues in this case—one was the cause of death, and the second was determining who murdered Esther Castellani. "To a certain extent, evidence overlaps on these two issues because the person who murdered Esther Castellani must have had access to her throughout the full period of time from January to July," said Toy. "The defence counsel was perfectly within his rights to make the submission that Mrs Luond was a liar. But because he makes it one, two, three, and four times in an extremely loud voice shouldn't influence you in your deliberations. I suggest to you there was a substantial quantity of arsenic still in that bowl and that Mr Castellani was very anxious to make sure nobody else got a mouthful."

Toy reminded the jury that Rene had told friends and co-workers that his wife's illness was caused by weed killer or insecticide while his mistress was telling people of their plans to marry—twelve days before Esther died.

In his instructions to the jury, Justice Dryer told them that they must not infer that Rene was the sort of person likely to commit the crime because of his character. He told them that motive, no matter how strong, could not by itself prove a crime. He added that members of the victim's own family or her friends had an opportunity to feed her arsenic as well as her husband. "Any one of them might have been doing it, even at her request," he said, and left them to consider the possibility that she'd given herself the arsenic.

Dryer told them: "There are two aspects of the matter that you have got to consider. You have got to rule out an accidental death. You have got to rule out suicide, and then you have got to look around and you've got to find, on the evidence, who did it, and I suggest to you on the evidence before you, that there is only one conclusion, that is, that it was the accused Rene Emile Castellani."

The jury did not believe Maclean's spirited defence or the idea that someone other than Rene had motive and opportunity to murder Esther. They did not consider the possibility that she gave herself arsenic over a seven-month period, particularly that she did so while paralyzed in a hospital bed.

The jury deliberated for just over six hours, including a two-hour break for dinner. When they returned with their verdict, Castellani sat in the prisoner's dock with his arms folded and showed no emotion. As the foreman pronounced him guilty, he let his head drop forward, then he raised it again to listen to Justice Dryer pronounce the death sentence.

Reporters noted that "blonde thirty-eight-year-old Gloria Yusep," sitting in the front row, as she had throughout the trial, buried her head in her hands and cried as the verdict was read.

The jury then took five minutes to decide that Rene would not get a recommendation for clemency.

Asked if he had anything to say, Rene said, "I have been asked three or four times if I was guilty of killing my wife. I did not kill my wife." He then turned his head to look at the jury and said, "May God have mercy on your souls." Some of the jury members actually recoiled, *Vancouver Sun* columnist Denny Boyd reported. "Rene could still play a role."

Rene was sentenced to hang on January 23, 1968.

One of the jury members was stopped by a reporter as he left the courthouse. He admitted that the trial had been "a painful experience. We went over and over and over all the evidence while we were deliberating to see if there was any reasonable doubt about the accused being guilty. We could not find it," he said.

CHAPTER 21
DEATH ROW

The day after Rene was sentenced to hang, the headlines changed, and this time Jeannine was the focus. The night the trial ended, she told Lolly she was going ice-skating with some friends from school, but they were actually going to a party. Jeannine and two other girls were walking down the street at around 8:30 p.m. when Jeannine started to cross the road. She was hit by a police car driven by Corporal Ronald Foyle, who was giving chase to a traffic offender.

The roads were slippery and visibility was poor because of heavy rain. The siren on Foyle's patrol car was not operating at the time, and Foyle admitted to travelling at "slightly above the speed limit." In the report, Foyle said, "I was pursing a traffic violator on 54th. On approaching Gladstone, I saw a pickup truck coming west. As he passed the intersection, I saw the girls. I couldn't distinguish where they were going. I hit the brakes, and the vehicle went out of control and hit one of them."

Jeannine was thrown ninety-five feet (thirty metres) and when she landed had a broken arm, leg, and pelvis, and her eyelid was torn off. She was rushed to Vancouver General Hospital.

"It was just a freak accident," says Jeannine. "They didn't know if I was going to live."

She was in hospital for more than a month and had to spend her fourteenth birthday there. Her father's appeal to be let out of jail to visit her was rejected, and her only visitors were her father's lawyers, Lolly, and a couple of friends from school.

Three days after the accident, Jeannine woke up to find a dozen red roses from Corporal Foyle. She clearly remembers Albert Mackoff,

Castellani Girl Injured

The 13-year-old daughter of convicted poison murderer Rene Castellani was seriously injured Saturday when she was hit by a police car.

Jeannine Castellani, 6331 Argyle, a witness for her father at his trial for murder of her mother, Esther, is in satisfactory condition in Vancouver General Hospital.

Police said the girl suffered a broken arm, broken leg and face cuts when she was thrown 95 feet by a police car driven by Cpl. Ronald Foyle.

Police said Foyle was chasing a traffic violator east on Fifty-fourth about 8:30 p.m. when the girl apparently ran into the roadway at Gladstone.

Roads were slippery and visibility was poor due to a heavy rain.

Deputy Chief Constable John Fisk said the warning equipment on Foyle's patrol car was not in operation at the time and Foyle was travelling at just "slightly above the speed limit."

In the report Foyle said:

"I was pursuing a traffic violator on Fifty-fourth. On approaching Gladstone, I saw a pickup (truck) coming west.

"As he passed the intersection, I got a glimpse of some girls. With the bright lights and rain I couldn't distinguish where they were going. I hit the brakes and the vehicle went out of control and hit one of them."

Jeannine was thrown about 95 feet after being hit.

Her two companions, who were walking behind her, were not involved in the accident.

Castellani wept when he was told of his child's injuries by a deputy warden at Oakalla.

Lawyer Charles Maclean, who represented Castellani at his

JEANNINE CASTELLANI
. . . arm, leg broken

recent trial, said he and lawyer Albert Mackoff visited Castellani at the prison Sunday and found that he was "very, very upset."

"He (Castellani) knows this was a very unfortunate accident and he would like to see, if at all possible, the officer (Foyle) to reassure him of this," said Maclean.

Maclean said that he, Mackoff and Mrs. Lollie Miller, a key figure in the Castellani trial, have been given authority by the convicted murderer to act on the child's behalf.

When asked if Castellani would request permission to visit his daughter, Maclean said the subject had not yet been discussed.

He said such permission involved a lengthy legal process and would have to be given by the sheriff of New Westminster who has custody of Castellani.

On the night following her father's conviction for capital murder, Jeannine Castellani was hit by a police car and spent more than a month in the hospital. (*Vancouver Sun*, October 10, 1967)

her dad's first lawyer, coming to visit. He'd asked Lolly to find out what Jeannine would like. Jeannine told her she wanted a pair of brown leather penny loafers, and Mackoff bought them for her.

While in hospital, Jeannine had to learn to walk again. And when she finally got out, Lolly threw her a surprise party. "I remember her being excited. She brought me to the house in the car and everybody was there," says Jeannine. "It was really nice of her because I didn't have friends over very often."

In April 1968, Rene had his lawyer John Davies file a lawsuit in the Supreme Court on Jeannine's behalf seeking damages from the City of Vancouver for her accident.

Even though he was now on death row for the murder of her mother, Rene retained custody of Jeannine. Rene signed over his custodial rights to Lolly and kept a tight hold on Jeannine. She was not allowed to see anybody from Esther's side of the family. "My dad had told me that I was not to talk to my grandma and grandpa because they would take me away, and I would never see him again," said Jeannine. "He said, 'I mean it, Jeannine. You have to promise me that.'" She said her grandparents would leave boxes of clothing or other presents for her at the school office, and she would often see them driving near the school and driving down the alley behind their house.

"I would see them, and I would just start running in the opposite direction, screaming because I was so scared they were going to kidnap me and I'd never see my dad or my new family again. He had made them out to be really bad people," she said. "One day, I was hanging up laundry and they drove up the laneway behind my house. I ran in the house calling 'Lolly, Lolly!' I missed them dearly, but I was afraid of them at the same time." Jeannine now believes that being kept away from Esther's family was her father's way of keeping her under control, even from jail.

Less than two weeks before he was scheduled to hang, Rene was one of sixteen people to have their death sentence commuted by Prime Minister Lester Pearson's federal government. Rene was now facing a mandatory life sentence without eligibility for parole until he had served twenty-five years.[20]

Charles Maclean continued to work on Rene's second appeal, which was finally heard in July 1968. Maclean argued that the evidence against his client was not sufficient to warrant his conviction for the murder of his wife. He also submitted that Justice Dryer misdirected the jury, failed to adequately explain the evidence given by Sheila Luond, and allowed certain admissions of a "gossipy nature" about Rene's affair with Lolly that were irrelevant and highly prejudicial to his client.

20　In 1967, the Government of Canada passed legislation temporarily suspending the death penalty for all crimes of murder except the killing of a police officer or a prison guard in the execution of their duties. During this trial period, all death sentences for murder were automatically commuted. The last executions in Canada were in December 1962, when Ronald Turpin and Arthur Lucas were hanged in Toronto for separate murders.

Although the three Court of Appeal justices agreed that the trial judge might have harmed Castellani's case by refusing to allow his lawyers to admit certain evidence, they felt that the refusal was not prejudicial and there was no substantial wrong or miscarriage of justice.

The appeal focused on the circumstantial evidence that was the foundation of the case. The chief concern for the three justices was that two long and highly publicized trials that highlighted the affair between Rene and Lolly, as well as his lies, would have brought about an emotional verdict from the jury. The other concern was that much of the Crown's proof came from the recollections of witnesses from years before, as well as testimony from Esther's family, both of which would possibly have been coloured by their hatred of Rene.

The circumstantial evidence, they ruled, was sufficient to sustain the conviction. With the exception of the nine-day BowMac promotion, Rene had the opportunity to feed his wife arsenic during her whole illness, including the seven weeks that she was in hospital.

He had motive to kill his wife so that he could remarry, and he had the knowledge to do so. He knew that his wife was going to die shortly, even though the doctors had not told him that, and he told several colleagues that her illness could have been caused by a weed killer or insecticide, and a can of commercial weed killer containing arsenic, with a missing portion, was found in his home.

Now that his second appeal was squashed with no hope for an acquittal, Rene was transferred from Burnaby's Oakalla Prison Farm to the Matsqui Institution in Abbotsford. Matsqui had opened in 1966 and was built to hold 312 inmates, many in treatment for drug addiction.

Rene had lucked out again—it was a progressive medium-security prison.

CHAPTER 22
LIVING WITH LOLLY

Followers of the Castellani murder case have wondered, over the decades, whether Lolly Miller was complicit in Esther's murder or she was just another of Rene's victims. Unfortunately, it's impossible to know for certain. When she met Rene, she was a twenty-five-year-old single mother with a full-time job. Rene was a charismatic, handsome minor celebrity, and she was quite probably flattered by his attention.

Lolly was forced to resign from CKNW because of the affair, but, ironically, Rene was able to keep his job because he had a sick wife. She was dragged through the media and put on the stand at the inquest. Later, with her lover on death row, she was left to raise his thirteen-year-old child with no financial support from Rene or his family. She could easily have played the evil stepmother, but today, Jeannine feels no ill will toward her.

"I can honestly say that Lolly was never mean to me when I lived there," says Jeannine. "My friends said they didn't find her very warm and fuzzy. I don't know, I didn't find many of my friends' parents warm and fuzzy. It was a different era back then."

Author Merrilee Robson does remember a warm side to Lolly. As a child, she lived across the street from the Millers in Coquitlam when Lolly was married to her first husband. "My little brother used to play with Don. Lolly was younger than my parents and quite pretty. I remember clearly that she gave me a kimono-style housecoat with butterflies all over it. It must have been something she didn't want anymore. But I remember that it was the most glamorous thing I'd ever owned, and I was thrilled that she'd given it to me. So I have quite fond memories of her and was sad when the scandal came out later."

Jeannine attended David Thompson Secondary (shown here in the 1960s) between 1967 and 1969. (Courtesy Vancouver School Board)

Jeannine remembers that Lolly loved to hula dance. "I remember her hula dancing in the living room, and she could really sway those hips, let me tell you," she says. Lolly's son, Don, recently told Jeannine that his mother used to teach dance, so "that makes sense now," says Jeannine. Some Sundays Lolly would take Don to his grandparents and she and Jeannine would go to Abbotsford to visit Rene at the Matsqui prison. "I don't remember a whole lot of visits with her. Rene and Lolly were pretty lovey-dovey, so I really didn't have much of a visit with my dad, and I probably sometimes didn't even go with her," says Jeannine.

Lolly would often have Jeannine babysit Don, and Jeannine remembers getting on well with Lolly's mother and stepfather, Augie and Marlo Giuliani.

"I don't really remember anything bad about living with Lolly," says Jeannine. "If I did something wrong, I was grounded, and it was for a long time. My dad was in jail, I had been hit by a car—I try to think about her situation, and I don't know what I would have done in her place."

The worse thing that Jeannine remembers is "coming home from school one day, and I said, 'Where's Cocoa?'" the little brown poodle that her mother and aunt Gloria had given her the Christmas before Esther died. "And Lolly said, 'Cocoa had cancer, and we had to put her down.' Lolly didn't tell me that the dog was sick." But Lolly's cat had had four kittens, and after Cocoa's death, she gave one to Jeannine and one to Don.

Once, when Jeannine had been in trouble at school, she was sent home with her punishment. "I remember this vividly," she says. "I had to write 'Patience is a virtue. I must behave,' one hundred times because I was probably in trouble again for talking out loud, and that's what you used to have to do. I was in the kitchen writing my lines, and I heard what I thought was water running. I thought that was weird, and I looked outside and our garage was on fire. I thought it must have been Don playing with matches."

Over half a century later, Don told her she was right. He'd been playing with matches, and the garage at the back of the house burned down. Don says he would have been about seven. Jeannine lost every-thing that Rene had stored in there for her, including Paul McCartney's autograph from the Beatles concert.

"Rene had all these old, old records," says Don. "I remember we used to take them outside and chuck them at the side of the garage like Frisbees."

"There were boxes and boxes of them," says Jeannine.

I asked Don what he knew of his father, who'd died when he was a baby. Don says that whenever he would ask Lolly about him, she would say, "I should have divorced him."

Don Miller in 1963, age four. (Courtesy Don Miller)

Lolly started to work different shifts and was away from home a lot. Either Jeannine babysat Don or he would stay with his grandparents, who lived in Burnaby. Jeannine had made a lot of friends at her new school and was now in grade ten—a fifteen-year-old with too much time on her hands. It was 1969. She drank but didn't do drugs.

"LSD was really big back then, and a lot of my friends were experimenting with it," she says. "I remember being with girlfriends and getting them home on the bus because they were high. People would buy it right in front of the Agrodrome. It was really easy to get and cheap. I was like the little mother goose, getting them home."

Jeannine says her curfew was seven p.m. during the week and ten p.m. on weekends. The first time she had sex was in the late 1960s, when she was thirteen or fourteen. "I met a boy at the new school I went to. We did not use condoms or have birth control pills. I wasn't promiscuous—or I guess I was. I always knew the person, and I just thought it was what you did. I never really thought about it."

One of Jeannine's closest friends from school was Carol Schmautz.

Her parents often let Jeannine stay overnight, and, oddly, Carol's mother, June, had served on the jury at Rene's inquest. She knew all about Jeannine's history, but she didn't tell Jeannine this until she was much older. Carol remembers Lolly well (especially her long hair and her love of her cats) and says that she was very demanding of Jeannine. "She would make Jeannine scrub black scuff marks on the kitchen floor, and Jeannine was always babysitting Lolly's son, Don." Carol says, though, that Jeannine never seemed to mind looking after Don. Her friends would go to Lolly's to hang out and watch television.

One night in 1969, when Don was at his grandparents and Jeannine was supposed to be staying at Carol's, the two girls met up with a couple of boys they liked from school. "We were just wandering around, and I said, 'You know, no one is home at my house. Let's go there.' So we did." Jeannine and Carol were stunned when a man they had never seen before came home with Lolly. "That's when I knew Lolly was seeing somebody else," says Jeannine.

Carol says she vividly remembers that night. "That was a very awkward situation. She was supposed to be in love with Jeannine's dad."

Lolly was furious with Jeannine. "All hell broke loose," says Jeannine. "I was grounded." She wasn't allowed to go anywhere except to school and home. A few days later, a big black Buick pulled up, driven by her aunt Rose—Rene's sister. Jeannine's bags were packed and put in the trunk, and she was taken to live in North Vancouver.

Jeannine doesn't remember talking to her father about Lolly's new boyfriend. But if Rene was upset about being dumped by Lolly, he never mentioned it to his daughter. "I believe that Lolly must have told my dad. Then he must have made the arrangements for his sister Rose to take me. I don't remember any discussion of Lolly from my dad after that. Honestly, I don't think it was that big of a deal. He would say, 'It

Lolly Miller, bottom row, third from left, April 1959. (Courtesy Don Miller)

will be fine. It will be you and me, don't worry. You behave yourself and don't get into trouble, and I'll get parole and we'll be a family again."

She'd been living with Lolly and Don for more than four years and considered them family. Jeannine never saw Lolly again, and it would be almost fifty years before she was reunited with Don.

She didn't even get to take her kitten.

In 1970, when Don was ten, Lolly married Ron Fairweather, an inspector at the meat packing plant where they both worked. They never again spoke of Jeannine or what happened to her. It was, says Don, as if she'd died. The new family moved to White Rock after Don's stepfather became a customs officer, and Don remembers a childhood of being bullied by his older, much bigger stepbrother. Don moved in with his grandparents as soon as he graduated from high school and has not seen or heard from his mother since 2008. He told me that he thinks his mother is "evil," that he doesn't know or care whether she is alive or dead, and that she should never have had children.

Although Lolly may not have been involved in planning Esther's murder, it's hard to imagine that she stayed clueless after hearing the evidence against Rene at the inquest and reading it on the front page of every newspaper. "Lolly would have had suspicions, and she probably believed he did it," says forensic psychologist Dr Burke. "I think he was being pressured by Lolly to move on." It may have become too difficult for Rene to keep both his wife and mistress happy. He'd already moved Esther to a larger home and the final straw may have been Lolly losing her job over allegations of the affair. She could have put pressure on Rene and caused him to speed up the timeline for his wife's murder. This could account for the mistakes he made along the way, such as applying for a mortgage with Lolly in their "married" names while Esther was still alive, says Burke. "Maybe something changed in the relationship, and Lolly started to demand more from him," says Burke. "It could be that Lolly was putting pressure on him to leave his wife because of her own financial situation and wanting to buy a house. He just wanted what he wanted, and he wasn't willing to settle or make any sacrifices."

Burke says it's possible that, at least in the early stages, Rene wasn't trying to murder his wife, just make her sick enough so that she wouldn't question his whereabouts and he could spend more time with Lolly. When he fooled the family doctor, and then a string of specialists, he probably became emboldened and decided to remove her permanently. Poison would have seemed a clever way to kill his wife because Esther had acknowledged she had unhealthy eating habits, and it was easy to blame her for her own illness.

After Rene was sent to jail, Lolly may have found that taking in Jeannine was unavoidable, suggests Burke. "It was a time when people tried to do their duty, and maybe she felt a duty to him." Or her motives may have been more practical than altruistic. "He may have made her promise to take care of his daughter and keep her away from her family. Lolly may have been afraid that if she did mistreat Jeannine, it would come back on her somehow."

Jeannine's aunt Rose had a beautiful house and two adopted children. Jeannine hated living there. Her name was changed to MacIlroy, and she was enrolled at Delbrook Senior Secondary in the middle of grade ten and told not to talk to anybody about her past. "I was cut off from everybody. They wouldn't allow me to talk to any of my friends that I'd made at David Thompson," says Jeannine.

"I was really upset when Jeannine was taken away, and I made my dad drive me to North Vancouver to see her," says Carol. "Rose opened the door, and she asked me what I was doing there. I said, 'I need to see Jeannine,' and Jeannine was standing on the staircase—I could see her—and Rose shut the door in my face. I was devastated. That was my best friend, and she wouldn't let me see her."

The one good thing that came out of living with Rose, says Jeannine, is that her aunt reunited her with her maternal grandparents. "That was very kind of her. I would sometimes go and spend the weekend at my grandparents' like I did when I was little. We'd go to the bakery and grandma would make dinner. I'd help her with the laundry in her wringer washing machine. They were really good times. My aunt Gloria came back into my life, and I would spend weekends at her place."

The only problem for Jeannine was that Gloria and her grandparents refused to talk about Esther. "My grandmother would instantly start crying, so I would change the subject. It was just a place I couldn't go."

Her aunt Gloria and her uncle Karl had told Jeannine stories about their father's violent temperament. And when Jeannine's cousin became pregnant at age sixteen, she later told Jeannine that their grandfather Karl hit her, called her a slut and a whore, and locked her in a room. But Jeannine only witnessed his anger once. When she had asked him if her mother ever knew that he was not her real father. "Then I saw his anger, and it scared me. He was furious," she says. "He said, 'She was like a daughter to me. Don't you ever, ever say that.' He just went nuts."

Jeannine has a difficult time reconciling the allegations—made separately by both Gloria and Esther's brother, Karl—that her grandfather molested her mother. It was especially difficult for her given that her mother had often let her stay overnight by herself with her grandparents. "When I found out my mum was sexually abused by him, that just sickened me. I used to say to my kids, 'How could my mum and dad let me stay with them by myself?' I couldn't understand how my mum could do that," she says. "But things back in those days were so different. Everything was shoved under the carpet."

Dr Heather Burke says it's quite common for victims of sexual abuse and incest to compartmentalize their feelings. "It could be that because she was older when the abuse occurred, [Esther] didn't think that it could happen to her young daughter." She may not have been able to believe "that her father could do that to somebody else. That's not uncommon," says Burke. "It also depends on how Esther interpreted the abuse. It could be very muddled in her head with the affection that she had for her father. She may have blamed herself and not wanted to lose her family—just sweep it all under the rug—it happens a lot. She may have had a huge level of denial about what had happened to her. Particularly back then, people didn't talk about it."

The other thing that puzzles Jeannine is why her grandparents and her aunt Gloria did not fight Rene and Lolly for custody of her. Burke thinks it may have been because Rene was aware of Esther's sexual abuse by her father. Mabel and Karl might have been worried that a custody battle would reveal some of their ugly family secrets. "The family violence, the abuse—they were probably worried that he would spill the beans, and that was not something they could take the chance on," she says.

As soon as Jeannine graduated from high school, the Schmautzes decided that they needed to get her out of her aunt's house, where she'd been so unhappy. They took Jeannine to visit Rene in Abbotsford, where he was out on a day pass and working at a local fair, and asked him if Jeannine could come and live with them.

"I remember sitting at the picnic table and Mum and Dad asking him to allow Jeannine to come and live in our home. Of course he had lots of questions because he didn't know us," says Carol. "He was looking out for her, and he knew that she wasn't happy. He gave permission for her to come and live in our home. He wanted her to be happy."

Gloria came to get her things and move her from Rose's to the Schmautzes'. Jeannine never saw Rose again.

Jeannine paid forty-eight dollars a month to the Schmautzes' for room and board. "I could have my friends over, food—it was like my own house, and I felt at home there," she says. "I would come home from work, and Mrs Schmautz would be sitting there smoking her cigarette in her cigarette holder. She was an at-home mum, and Carol's dad really had a soft spot for me."

Jeannine had started working at BC Rail during grade twelve through a work experience program. After graduation, she stayed as the mail girl. Soon afterward, her grandmother used her connections to get Jeannine a job with BC Tel. She started there in December 1971.

Carol says that her family would often take Jeannine out to Abbotsford to visit Rene at Matsqui. "He was always so happy to see her and sad to see her go." Rene even showed Jeannine and Carol his cell. "I just remember it was clean. It wasn't like the prisons that you see on television," she says. "Nobody talked behind glass windows. Jeannine could hug her dad."

For many years, Jeannine didn't believe that her father was responsible for her mother's death, and her friends shielded her from the media. "You are never going to think your dad is going to do something like that," says Carol. "We stood by her. We never said, 'Hey, you need to read this,' because that would have hurt her."

The following December, the Schmautzes took Jeannine to see a play that Rene was performing in at Matsqui, and the following week, he would spend Christmas at their home. It was his first full weekend pass out of jail, just five years after sentencing.

After someone from the prison dropped him off, a woman turned up on the Schmautzes' doorstep. "He said, 'Oh, this is my friend,'" says Carol. "Mum and Dad were not happy, but they accepted it for Jeannine's sake. They truly loved her like a daughter." The woman had left by the time the girls woke up in the morning, and Jeannine took her father to another friend's house for Boxing Day.

Carol says she liked Rene. "He was Jeannine's father, and when he was there he was good to her, and she was happy to have him there. When he came to visit in our home, it was nice to see Jeannine so happy that her dad was there, and they did stuff together. I remember [a time when] we took him to the store, and he got a bunch of French bread and pizza sauce and made pizza bread."

Jeannine continued to visit Rene frequently. Sometimes one of her cousins would drive her; sometimes she took the bus. Once, Rene asked her to take the bus to Cultus Lake and spend the weekend with him. When she arrived, she found that he was staying with a woman she hadn't met before.

"I started to see my dad in a whole different way, and I was uneasy about him," she says. "He had a lot of women in his life. He never talked about my mum, and he never put his arms around me and said, 'I didn't do it.' He never did. That's all I wanted to hear."

Performance of *Tower Circus*, a play presented at the Matsqui Institution by the Institutional Theatre Productions. (Courtesy the Reach Gallery Museum, September 21, 1977)

CHAPTER 23
VISITING HOURS

In January 1973, Jeannine, now nineteen, moved out of the Schmautzes'
into a basement suite with a friend. One night, they went to a dance
near their home, where Jeannine saw the young guy she had been dating
with a girl she worked with at BC Tel. "I was absolutely heartbroken—it
wasn't a good night," she said. Upset and shocked, she told her friends
that she needed to get some air and was going to walk home. She got
partway there when she noticed that somebody was following her.

"I started to pick up the pace, and I scooted between two houses,"
she says. "He got me from behind and said, 'Don't scream, don't move,
or I'm going to hurt you.' He had a leather coat on, I could feel it, and
I'm thinking in my head, *Okay, is it somebody from the dance? Who is it?*
I was so scared. He was so out of breath. I don't know if it was because
he was sexually excited or from running. There were lights on in the
house, but I was too scared to scream. He told me not to turn around,
and I didn't. He said, 'I'm not going to hurt you if you just do what I
want you to do.' He tried from behind but couldn't get it up, and I had
to masturbate him off. It was all over my hands. I never saw his face."

Jeannine went home and had a bath and scrubbed herself raw. "I
didn't want to go to the police because I had nothing to tell them. I
never saw him. I know people say that you're supposed to kick and
scream, but I went into survival mode. You do what you have to do," she
said about the sexual assault. "I wasn't afraid of anything before that."

The next day, she put in a call to her dad in prison. "He said he
didn't want the police involved, he didn't want it in the papers," says
Jeannine. "My dad had me believing that if I did anything wrong out
in the world, that would jeopardize his parole. It would jeopardize

him and me being together. It would jeopardize everything. I wasn't perfect out there, but I always tried to stay under the radar."

The following weekend, Rene visited Jeannine on a weekend pass, and he brought the same woman she had met at the Schmautzes' and a box of maraschino chocolates. As her father requested, Jeannine didn't go to the police and they did not talk about it again.

Jeannine and her friends used to hang out at No. 5 Orange at Main and Powell streets. It was a strip club during the day, and still is, but in the 1970s it turned into a disco at night with a deejay. On the first night she'd been out since the attack, one of Jeannine's friends saw a guy she knew, and soon they were all sharing a table. Jeannine ended up talking to Dale. He invited her and her friend to a party the following night. The party was thrown by a girl Jeannine had gone to school with and was well attended by many old friends. "When I met Dale, he wasn't like the others. He was a really nice guy, a real gentleman," she says. "That's what attracted me to Dale. He really liked me."

When Rene was first incarcerated, the prison system followed the medical model, which viewed criminals as physically or mentally ill but able to be cured and rehabilitated with medical procedures, drugs, and therapy. "It was all about the treatment of offenders," says VPD inspector Earl Andersen, author of *Hard Place to Do Time*. "They really tried everything. There were lobotomies and plastic surgeries and experiments with mind-altering drugs. You name it."[21]

In 1970, the British Columbia provincial legislature passed the

---

21   According to Andersen, in the 1950s and '60s, Dr Guy Richmond, senior medical officer at Oakalla Prison Farm, performed more than 600 surgeries on prisoners, from basic rhinoplasty operations to reshaping jaws and ears to removing scars and tattoos, to help them rehabilitate upon release. Earl Andersen, *Hard Place to Do Time: Oakalla Prison, 1912–1991* (New Westminster, BC: Hillpointe Publishing, 1993), 72.

Correction Act, which phased out the old medical model and introduced the reintegration model, which took the view that prisoners
were responsible for their crimes and needed help to re-enter society.

Brian William Slaney was a twenty-year-old drug addict with a
juvenile record who had been caught stealing prescription pads from
Montreal General Hospital. When he was sent to Matsqui in 1970, he
found some of the old system in place with twice weekly therapy for
groups of twenty-five inmates and access to psychiatrists, therapists,
and prison psychologists. According to Slaney, under the new system of
reintegration, prisoners were evaluated every three months, rewarded
for their good behaviour, and given grades that determined how much
money was put into their "canteen" and what privileges they were given.
Prisoners had their own cells, which contained a bed, a toilet, and a
small desk. By the end of his sentence, Slaney was allowed to finish
grade twelve at the local high school. "I got out [of prison] at eight in
the morning, walked to the public high school, and took classes with
the teenagers. I had to be back at 4:30 every night," he says.

Slaney also says he managed to get a fairly steady supply of heroin,
using two or three times a week. "There were 260 drug addicts in one
place. They are going to find ways to get it," he says. Rene was one of
the few prisoners not incarcerated for a drug conviction and not in
the drug program. "Rene kept to himself, which proved to work in
his favour," says Slaney. "I remember him walking around with files
in his hand. He was quite a tall guy, and he was kind of brusque and
businesslike, but he was always ready to laugh at a joke, even if it
wasn't funny."

One of the privileges of being a Grade 4—the highest level of
freedoms for inmates—was that prisoners didn't have their cell doors
locked and could go to the library when they wanted. Slaney says
rewards were based on how the inmate conducted himself in the prison

Rene, on a temporary absence from Matsqui, with Jeannine,
circa 1976

setting and were not related to the crime that they were incarcerated for. When he arrived, Slaney says, Rene had already reached the Grade 4 level and was receiving temporary absences so that he could go out and work in the community.

"They were really trying to make new people out of us," he says. "They wanted us to be social and expand our avenues and to talk to people and become different."

Most of the prisoners worked out in the gym or played handball and other sports, but Rene stayed away, says Slaney. "He wasn't one of us. If anything, he was down the ladder." Clever at adapting to new situations, Rene knew to keep his head down, get out of prison and into the community as much as he could, and do his time as quickly and quietly as possible.

Hal Davis, CKNW's program manager, remembered running into Rene and a prison guard in Abbotsford one day. He was surprised that Rene was getting day passes so soon into his life sentence. Rene told him he had organized a prison band called the Hangman's Five.[22]

Dianna Buehler grew up in Abbotsford and worked in the prison system for thirty years. She didn't start until after Rene was paroled, but she remembers him well when he first got day parole and was working at a non-profit organization where she volunteered. "I knew quite a few of the inmates," she says. "Some videotaped local hockey games that kids were playing in and put it on the local channel. For a lot of inmates, it was an excellent way to get new skills."

Buehler says that everybody seemed to like Rene, as he was very personable. While he was on parole, he worked with Community Services, a non-profit organization that helped single parents and people on low incomes and held Christmas parties and summer camps

---

22 Davis, *Top Dog!*, 82.

for kids whose parents couldn't otherwise afford to have them go. One year, Rene played Santa Claus, says Buehler, who has pictures of her kids sitting on his lap. "He really was a great Santa Claus because he had the personality," she says. "My mum and I used to laugh because nobody knew that he was in prison, and all these people just loved him."

Later, when he started work at CFVR Abbotsford while living in the pre-release centre at Matsqui, he became known as Rene the Roadrunner because he did the radio station's traffic reports. He also drove around town in a station wagon, passing out promotional gifts from the station. He would stop by Buehler's house and deliver records and other prizes from the contests that her mother used to enter regularly.

I mentioned to Buehler that Jeannine had told me Rene was often out with different women on his weekend passes from jail. "That wouldn't surprise me," she said. "A lot of the inmates that got out on these day passes would be out for maybe four or five hours during the week. They met a lot of women and the women liked them. And it's still that way. We still have women marrying prisoners."

Buehler says that it was a much smaller jail in those early days, and prisoners got plenty of individual attention. As long as their visitors passed a screening, the jail was quite flexible with visitations. "They could have as many as wanted to come," she says. "I would assume Rene had quite a few." Rene's work with Community Services put him in an ideal place to find "responsible" women who could sponsor him to get him out of jail on the weekends. These were probably a few of the women Jeannine met.

Walter Paetkau, former executive director of Community Services, says Rene and another inmate named Don Anderson, who was rumoured to be a gunrunner in Central America, were the first to volunteer in January 1971 as part of the temporary absence program, which tried to connect inmates with the community and involve them in volunteer and civic activities. "I was responsible for him while he was engaged in volunteer activities several times a week. We respected each other and became friends," says Paetkau. "I visited him in prison on a fairly regular basis."

In 1973, after Anderson had escaped from jail (and taken the cash from the thrift store where he volunteered), Matsqui cracked down on temporary absences. Letters poured in from various organizations pleading that they reconsider. D.J. Smith, of the Waddell's Haven Guest Home for people with mental illnesses, wrote to say that Rene had supplied a prison band for a fundraising event and once organized an Italian dinner evening. Mrs. A.I. Allen, a social worker with the Mental Health Centre in Maple Ridge, wrote to thank Rene for his work. "Staff do not know how they could have managed without your help and enthusiasm, plus your sense of responsibility and 'going the extra mile,'" she told him. "Rene is so much a part of Christmas Bureau," wrote Flo Kenyon. "He has not only done more than his share, he's an inspiration to all of us who have worked with and for him. He brings out the best in us."

Rene was soon back in the community, doing public relations for various non-profit groups and volunteering at CFVR, where he also coordinated the station's broadcast activities for the Abbotsford air show every August.

Stephen Duguid taught at Matsqui Institution through the University of Victoria prison education program between 1973 and 1980. He says that by the time he arrived, the medical model was seen as a dismal failure in terms of recidivism and rehabilitation and was largely discontinued in favour of different programs.

Duguid initially taught history and says the university program proved popular with inmates, allowing them to mix with idealistic and sometimes radical young university types. By 1975, he was teaching in the Matsqui theatre program. Duguid doesn't remember Rene but says a lot of the prisoners participated in the plays. "It is very possible that he could have been in one or more of the plays that we sponsored, since more than just our students were involved," says Duguid. "Each play was a major event of sorts, involving more than a month of work and several performances put on for fellow inmates and family and guests. There were female actors involved, and he would have had ample opportunities to mix with non-prisoners who were helping with productions."

Bob Singleton was the manager at CFVR in the 1970s, and he was also the chair of the Citizen Advisory Committee at Matsqui. Singleton had no qualms about hiring Rene for the promotions department and to do traffic reports, and Rene worked at CFVR from September 1, 1979, to April 30, 1981, initially while on day parole from the prison.

"He was a pretty darn good employee," says Singleton. "We never had any problems with him at all. He never was a threat to anyone in the community. He was an easy guy to like. Everybody liked him. He was just one of the gang." Singleton says that Rene told him many times that he had not murdered his wife. "He said there were people in Vancouver who could clear him, but they wouldn't come forward," says Singleton. "Now whether that is true, I don't know, but he said that on numerous occasions. He always pleaded his innocence, and he didn't make a big deal out of it, but when it came up, he said he didn't do it." Singleton also says he always went by the nickname Rene the Roadrunner, never by his last name. "He played it pretty cool. He didn't do anything that would draw huge attention to himself."

Dr Heather Burke says it's not uncommon for guilty people to start believing their own lies. "They are invested in portraying their innocence, and they will deny it until the day they die," says Burke.

"If his daughter had been at his death bed, he still likely would have denied it because he didn't want to take responsibility."

It's also quite possible that people who weren't familiar with the case would have believed him, she says, because they saw him as charming and funny and didn't see the other side of him. "He was a pathological liar, just a smooth operator who was irresponsible with money, a dreamer who liked the night life and wheeling and dealing. Ordinary life wasn't good enough for him," says Burke.

As Jeannine began to get serious about Dale, she started to take a closer look at her father. "Dale did not like my dad, and Dale was a wonderful man. He had a German shepherd, and his dog didn't like him either, and that was a big thing for Dale," she says. "I think my dad was feeling threatened by Dale."

Jeannine's aunt Gloria and her grandmother's sister Ida had clipped and saved the newspaper articles about her mother's death and kept them for Jeannine. For the first time, she read about her father's trials, and she began to believe that he may have murdered her mother. "I never told him that I read the articles. I never once told him that I thought he might have been the one," she says. "We never discussed anything like that."

In November 1973, when she turned twenty-one, Jeannine received the settlement from her car accident six years earlier. Her share was $19,000; the other $8,000 went to the lawyers. She took part of the money and bought a 1972 MGB sports car. She and Dale planned a road trip to Banff and Jasper. Rene had a weekend pass and asked them to visit him before they left for their trip. The address he gave them turned out to be a trailer park in Abbotsford. Rene was staying with yet another woman. Jeannine doesn't remember her name, just that she was young and had a small boy with a heart problem. There was an old garage at the back of the house, and Jeannine was surprised to see some of her childhood things in there. There was the doll crib that her father had made her when she was a little girl and some of her mother's china figurines. He didn't say how he had gotten them or where he had kept them over the years he'd been in prison, and Jeannine never saw them again.

That night, Rene made spaghetti for dinner, and Jeannine and Dale slept over in the living room. The next day, he told her that he was entitled to some of the money from her settlement. "He said I owed him some money, that he needed a car when he got out so we could be together. Dale said, 'You are not going to give him any money.'"

Dale always supported her decision to see her father and would drive her to the prison and wait in the car. But the visits weren't going well. Rene made it clear that he didn't like Dale, he was unhappy that Jeannine was starting to doubt him, and he was furious that Jeannine would not give him any money from her accident settlement.

One Sunday, after she had moved in with Dale, she was visiting Rene at Matsqui in a supervised group room. "Dad said, 'I want you to put your arms around my waist.'" Rene had folded up a note tied with string inside a slit he had cut in the waistband of his pants. He told her to pull out the note, keep it tight in her hand, and not open it until she left the prison.

"I was petrified that I would be caught with the note in the prison. I went home and unfolded it and it said, 'Dale is walking on very thin ice with me. You used to dance in the arms of stars and now you are nothing but a pub crawler' and it went on and on," she said. Rene also wrote that she should have been grateful that he came to see her after the rape and that he didn't get angry with her for being assaulted. "The letter didn't say he was going to hurt anybody, but I was fearful that he might do something, or that he might have somebody do it for him. We were scared."

Dr Heather Burke says that when Rene didn't get his way, his true colours showed. When Jeannine refused to give Rene money from her accident settlement, he resorted to threatening her and her fiancé. When she was sexually assaulted, he wasn't concerned with how it had affected her but with how it would look at his parole hearing. "It's always all about him," says Burke.

For the first time since her father's conviction, Jeannine stopped visiting him in jail. Not long afterward, she got a call from one of her father's former colleagues at CKNW. "He was very upset with me and said that I should be behaving myself because my dad wanted parole," says Jeannine. "I said, 'I don't think you understand. He gave me a threatening letter.'"

After serving less than ten years of his life sentence, Rene moved into a pre-release trailer on the grounds of Matsqui. It was the first step toward full parole. He worked at the radio station during the day and came back to Matsqui at night to do his own cooking and sleep in his own room. Parole officers were on-site, and he would regularly get weekend passes.

"On the surface, most of us would be repulsed by the fact that they let this guy out at all. But the parole board doesn't just look at the offence. They also look at a person's history," says *Hard Place to Do Time* author Earl Andersen. "Castellani was a businessman, and he had no criminal record previous to this, so besides the fact that he poisoned his wife to death with arsenic, compared to all these other extremely dangerous people [in the jail], he was a relatively model citizen."

In 1976, Dale drove Jeannine to the prison to see her father. He stayed in the car. After that visit, "I just stopped," she says. "I couldn't do it anymore. I just didn't want him in my life."

Rene at Jeannine's South Vancouver basement suite on day parole from Matsqui, circa 1976.

It was the last time she ever saw him.

Rene was released on full parole in May 1979. He never tried to contact Jeannine.

"That's how it is with psychopaths," says Dr Heather Burke. "If they want something in their life, they just cast people off and they see it as a means to an end. When Jeannine stopped doing what Rene wanted, she stopped serving a purpose. His thing was to cast people off if they weren't falling in line with what he wanted—like his wife."

CHAPTER 24
OUT OF JAIL

When Rene was about to be released from jail, he phoned CKNW station manager Bill Hughes and asked for his old job back. Hughes was flabbergasted, writes Chuck Davis in *Top Dog!* "You have to be joking!" he said. "After all the trauma you put this station through!"

Rene didn't miss a beat. He soon had a job as the promotions guy and remote engineer at CFVR radio, settled down in Abbotsford, a rural community about forty-four miles (seventy-one kilometres) from Vancouver. In late 1978, he married his second wife, Mary.

CKNW's George Garrett says the last time he saw Rene was in the late 1970s. "The shock I had," he says. "I was out at our radio station on our network in Abbotsford, and this tall guy comes through the door from the library and says, 'George, how are you?' I thought I saw a ghost. It was Rene. I'd thought he was still in prison."

Bill Nelson was a deejay and the musical director for CFVR. Rene the Roadrunner did the traffic reports on Nelson's morning show. "He was really big on the CB craze of the late 1970s and early '80s, and that's largely where the Rene the Roadrunner thing came from. When he did his traffic reports, he also kept in touch with truck drivers on the CB to get up-to-date information from the horse's mouth."

Nelson says it was common knowledge that Rene was a convicted murderer. "He and I got along fine. We were actually quite good friends. I was at Rene's second wedding." Nelson says Rene told everybody that he did not murder his wife, that police always looked first to the husband, and that they had failed to properly investigate his sister-in-law, who had "mental health issues."

"Coincidentally, my uncle was the head of security at Matsqui and he told me that there was no question in anybody's mind, including all of the Vancouver Police Department, about his guilt," says Nelson. "I trusted my uncle's judgment on most matters." Nelson says that although he feels Rene was probably responsible for Esther's murder, there were things in the trial that bothered him. Not disposing of the weed killer was one of them.

"He was a very intelligent man, and if he's going to plan something like that, why wouldn't he dispose of the evidence as he went along?" he says. "On the other hand, he wasn't smart enough to not go on a Disneyland vacation with his girlfriend just after his wife died."

Rene also worked closely with Ted Schellenberg at station CKLG, and when Schellenberg moved to Nanaimo, at the time a small town on Vancouver Island, to start a new radio station with Bob Adshead, he asked Rene to go with him.[23] "Rene certainly wasn't my choice, but we were looking for a jack of all trades—a handyman who could set up remote broadcasts—which was what he did in Abbotsford," says Adshead. "I was aware of Rene's background prior to hiring. Ted and I discussed the potential downside to his employment, but there were things Rene could help us do. I was generally impressed with Rene when we first met. The decision to hire him was a pretty easy one."

CKLG Nanaimo was a small start-up station with about fifteen employees who all wore several hats. Rene, says Adshead, was a friendly, happy-go-lucky individual and a positive influence around the station and on the staff. Rene was given the title "engineer" but took on multiple roles, including promotions. "He was just that kind of guy who would dig his

---

23   Ted Schellenberg left radio to become the Member of Parliament representing Nanaimo–Alberni in Brian Mulroney's conservative government after the 1984 election. Bob Adshead added another radio station in Nanaimo and expanded into Courtenay, Campbell River, Parksville, and Port Alberni. He sold all six stations to Jimmy Pattison in 2006.

heels in and do whatever was wanted," says Adshead. "He definitely was a colourful individual. He'd walk into a room, and it was pretty electric just because he wasn't afraid to say hello to anybody, smile and shake their hand, and just be a jovial kind of character. We didn't discuss his background, and it never became an issue to our employees. If you needed something done, he was our go-to person. No arguments. No delays."

Rene and his second wife socialized with people from the station but mostly kept to themselves, says Adshead. "She was a friendly, easygoing individual, and they were actually quite well suited. As I recall, she was quite a bit younger than Rene. [There was a severe global recession] in the early '80s, and I remember how she tried to land a job and found things difficult for some time."

Rene worked at the station until a few months before he died in 1982. Adshead says he didn't tell anyone he had pancreatic cancer but would occasionally miss work because of a "stomach problem", as he'd call it.

Around the end of 1981, Jeannine got a call from her cousin Jeanne, Rene's sister's daughter, who lived in Calgary, Alberta. His sister and her daughter remained firmly convinced of his innocence and, as Jeannine learned, had kept in close contact with her father after she had broken off all contact with him. Jeanne had travelled to Nanaimo to help take care of him when he could no longer work or look after himself.

It was a surprise to Jeannine. She hadn't seen or talked to her father for more than five years, and she didn't know that he was sick or that he'd moved to Vancouver Island. Jeannine had got on with her life. She married Dale in 1977, and their first daughter, Lindsay, was born in 1980. Jeannine thinks that when Rene knew that she no longer believed in him, he found somebody who did.

"Jeanne called me and told me that my dad was dying in a hospital in Victoria, and if I wanted to go to see him, she would take me," says Jeannine. 'I said I wanted to go because I thought he has nothing to lose now, maybe he'll tell me how my mum died.'"

She decided to travel to Nanaimo and try for a deathbed confession. But she was too late. Rene died on January 4, 1982. He was fifty-six.

Jeannine went to his funeral. After the service, she was standing outside the church looking at the white hearse when Rene's wife approached her. "She said, 'I don't know how much you loved him, but I loved him very much,' and she walked away."

Bill Nelson had stayed in touch with Rene when he moved to Nanaimo and was one of the pallbearers at Rene's funeral. Later he helped Mary sort through Rene's things. "He had a dozen large cardboard boxes full of framed certificates of appreciation from everybody from the Vancouver Police to Greenpeace for all of the good deeds that he had done while in radio. And that all went in the landfill." Nelson says he found Esther's sterling silver cigarette case when he was going through Rene's things. "[Mary] said, 'I don't want it, it's got Esther's name on it.' I got it as a souvenir of Rene," he says.

Although Jeannine's daughters, Lindsay and Ashley, knew the names of their maternal grandparents and had seen their photos, Jeannine had kept her family history to herself. That all changed in 1992, when twelve-year-old Lindsay was invited on a field trip to the Vancouver Police Museum. A friend of Jeannine's told her that Esther's murder was on display in the true-crime section of the museum, complete with photos and sensational newspaper headlines. Jeannine had no idea. Not wanting Lindsay to find out that way, she asked then-curator Joe Swan to cover up the exhibit, which she said he did grudgingly. When she was able to talk to Lindsay about it a few days later, Lindsay just looked at her and said, "Why didn't you tell us, Mum? It wasn't your fault."

"After that, it came out in the open, and I was relieved that everyone knew," says Jeannine.

A few years later, Jeannine's cousin Jeanne came to stay with her. She gave her two CDs that Rene had cut for his Calgary family when he was working at CFVR Abbotsford in 1978. On the cover of one of them there's a picture of Rene standing in front of the radio call sign, with the caption "Rene and the Magic Pond." The first track is labelled "ME!"

Except for Jack Cullen's bootlegged Beatles recording and a few tapes that Cullen kept of Rene as Klatu and the Dizzy Dialler, all of Rene's on-air work for CKNW was lost or thrown out when the station moved to Vancouver in 1996. It makes listening to Rene's voice nearly four decades later creepily fascinating. As Jeannine describes it, it's like listening to an old-style radio, the kind that was around before TV. Rene tells stories, sings, and plays a character called Spruce with a funny voice and a crazy laugh. He tells his Calgary family how much he misses them, that he loves them and can't wait to see them on his upcoming visit to Calgary. He also mentions God a lot.

Jeannine listened to the CDs for the first time in 2018.

"When I listen to this, I start to see through him. He's always somebody else, he's very seldom himself," she says. "What's heartbreaking to me is he is out living in this world, carrying on, when he is supposed to be in jail. And jail is like a hotel—and I get really upset about this, because it was like a frigging hotel for him in Matsqui.

"I'm listening to him and thinking, *Is this really a murderer playing this music and forgetting what he did?* He got out so soon. He went into jail in 1966, and this is 1978, and he's working in the Abbotsford community."

There's not one mention of Jeannine in the recordings.

"My dad was really talented. He could play music by ear and sing, he could fix anything. He made cribs and doll beds for me that were immaculate. Where did all that go wrong?" she says. "He had no remorse. He should have been hanged for what he did."

CHAPTER 25
THE PERFECT MURDER WEAPON

So many things have changed since 1965, when Rene murdered Esther Castellani. In that decade alone, there was a seismic shift in politics, culture, and the law—at least the law pertaining to divorce—and in later years, there have been leaps and bounds in forensics and crime-solving technology.

If the Castellanis had been born fifty years later and Rene Castellani had murdered his wife using arsenic in her food and milkshakes, would doctors have discovered it before she died? Would pathologists have discovered it after she died? And if they did, would Rene Castellani still have been convicted of murder?

Nikos Harris, a professor of law at the University of British Columbia who uses the Castellani trial in his evidence class, says it's still a case that could go either way. "It strikes me as a case that falls into that high degree of suspicion," he says. "Anything that's in the suspicion category is not proof beyond a reasonable doubt. The problem with a jury is we don't get their reasons."

With the proliferation of *CSI* television shows, mystery and true-crime books and podcasts, you don't need to be a detective or a scientist to have a basic understanding of poisons today. Little of this type of information was available to Rene Castellani in 1965; certainly, it wasn't possible to do an internet search to find out where to buy arsenic and how quickly it could kill someone. In the 1960s, not even most scientists had heard of neutron activation analysis, so it's unlikely

Esther and unidentified man on Granville Street, circa 1945.

that Rene was aware that this technology could detect the ingestion of arsenic in a timeline through Esther's hair and nails.

Douglas Lucas, retired director of the Ontario Centre of Forensic Sciences, speculated that Rene may have even approached Ted Fennell or Eldon Rideout at the city analyst lab posing as a novelist and seeking information for his mystery. Lucas says he used to get requests like that quite often.

Today there are more sophisticated methods and technologies to detect arsenic in the human body—the mass spectrometer has replaced neutron activation analysis in cases involving poisons or toxins. But then, as now, you can only find arsenic poisoning if you are specifically looking for it. As Dr Richard Beck, one of several specialists who consulted on Esther's case said: "Testing for arsenic just never crossed our minds."

Dr William Schreiber, the former medical director of the Provincial Toxicology Centre and consultant pathologist at Vancouver General Hospital, said that even today most laboratories don't measure toxic metals because they need special equipment to do it. "And here's the problem with a poisoning: If [Esther] wasn't taking prescribed or illicit drugs, if she didn't have any industrial or workplace exposure to substances that might make her sick, and if there was no reason to think that somebody was trying to kill her—why would you even think about arsenic?"

Rene would have had more chance getting caught using poison as a murder weapon in 1865 than a century later or even in 2018. In the 1700s and 1800s, arsenic was such a popular way of dispatching inconvenient relatives and enemies that the UK parliament passed the Arsenic Act of 1851, requiring all purchases of the poison to be monitored and logged. That requirement didn't make it over to Canada, where, in 1965, arsenic for killing rats, mice, and weeds was readily available at nurseries and hardware stores and, not too long before that, had been used in the treatment of venereal disease.

The 1944 movie *Arsenic and Old Lace* would have appealed to Rene, and he had access to the library, knowledge of chemistry, and he was smart—perhaps a little too smart. Had Esther been cremated or had Rene thrown away the murder weapon, he would most likely have gotten away with murder.

When Esther first got sick, her symptoms mirrored the stomach flu, and her doctor gave her medicine for nausea. When she got sick again, he put it down to "gastronomic misadventures," lectured her on unhealthy eating habits, and gave her a diet to follow. When she continued to have bouts of vomiting and diarrhea, he put it down to an otherwise "pleasant person" who overate rich foods, made a fuss about it, and made her over-solicitous husband get the doctor out in the middle of the night because his wife had an upset stomach.

I'm puzzled that Rene would be sloppy enough to have left the murder weapon in plain view under the kitchen sink and then allowed detectives to search his house. Perhaps he thought that they'd never catch on. Or if they did figure out Esther's real cause of death, he could make a case that she died as a result of inhaling the weed killer as she sprayed the dandelions in her backyard.

Dr Gary Andolfatto, attending physician and emergency department research director at North Vancouver's Lions Gate Hospital, says he has not seen arsenic toxicity in his practice and wouldn't necessarily think of it if a patient presented with those symptoms today. "One of the axioms that we use in the ED is that 'common things happen commonly,' or put another way, 'when you hear hooves, think horses, not zebras.' So this type of case could certainly be missed in any emergency department I know of," he says. "However, emergency departments only examine people in a single moment in time, not longitudinally. This person would likely have been referred to an internal medicine specialist for a second opinion. Still, I think this would be a pretty tough thing to diagnose."

I asked Dr Schreiber if, after being hospitalized, Esther would have been diagnosed faster today. "Probably not," he said. "Medicine can be very frustrating because, ultimately, it is a statistical game. Ninety-nine times out of a hundred, when I show up with a stomach ache and diarrhea, it really is gastroenteritis, and the hundredth time it is a toxic ingestion. There are plenty of cases where people die and they never figure out what it is," he says.

If Rene had refused to have Esther autopsied, the case might have stopped there. The hospital doctor needed permission from next of kin, and with no reason to suspect murder—the death didn't appear to be sudden, unexpected, or unnatural—says Mike Porteous, superintendent of Investigative Services for the VPD, there would have been no reason to get the coroner's service involved. "You have a long-term sick person who passes away because she was sick. Why would you do an autopsy?" says Porteous.

As in 1965, a hospital autopsy would be unlikely to uncover arsenic today. Routine toxicology testing usually focuses on prescription and recreational drugs and would not normally test for arsenic or other heavy metals unless there was a good reason to suggest they had been ingested.

"There are probably twenty cases like this where they never figured it out for every case they did," says Schreiber. "So if you are looking for a lesson out of all this, the lesson is arsenic is still a pretty good bet if you want to kill someone."

Don and Jeannine, 2018.

EPILOGUE

May 7, 2018

I met with Jeannine and her daughter Ashley on June 25, 2017—two Sundays after my book launch for *Blood, Sweat, and Fear*. We talked for hours. After I got home, I sent Jeannine an email with Don Miller's phone number. She couldn't wait and phoned him straight away.

They looked at their work schedules and family commitments and decided the first date they could meet was July 11. Jeannine didn't tell Don at the time, but July 11 was the date of her mother's death.

The offspring of the Castellanis and the Millers met at a Boston Pizza in Maple Ridge. Jeannine and her daughters, Ashley and Lindsay, arrived first and sat on one side of the booth and ordered sangria. Jeannine sat at the end because she wanted to see Don as soon as he came in. She knew who he was, she says, as soon as she saw his eyes. "He had a brush cut when he was little, and his eyes were a greeny-brown almond shape and droopy on the side."

"I was really excited," she says. "He was very nervous to meet us, but it was like we had known each other for a long time—it was very comfortable. We had an instant connection."

Nearly fifty years had passed since they had last seen or heard anything about each other. In that time, both had married and had two children—two girls for Jeannine, a boy and a girl for Don. Jeannine lost her husband, Dale, in 2005. Don and his wife, Debbie, lost their daughter, who like Jeannine's younger daughter was named Ashley, to the H1N1 virus.

"They showed me a photo of their grandson, and it was just how I remembered Don," she says. "I had all these questions written down and he answered every single one, and we both said at the very same time, 'Do you remember our address?' and we both said it at the same time, '6331 Argyle Street.' The most important question to me was how had he been? How was he?"

They talked about television shows they remembered watching over the more than four years they'd lived together as brother and sister. They talked about the trip to Disneyland with Rene and Lolly, taken the day after Esther's funeral. "He remembered more about the Disneyland trip than I did, and he was only six," she says. "He remembered us sleeping in the back of the company station wagon with sleeping bags. He remembered that he had nightmares and he would come to me and I would console him. That struck me to my heart—he came to me and not his mum.

"Don said that his life was really no better than mine at the end of the day. He felt like he and I were just left like two little dogs that nobody wanted."

Jeannine told Don that she'd worked at the Home Depot in Surrey for the past twenty years. He told her that he had recently retired as a carpenter for the school district of Coquitlam.

Jeannine and Don now talk on the phone a few times a month and have met up several times since that first lunch. The Millers dropped by on Christmas Day and they exchanged gifts, just like any regular family.

"Don tells me all the time that getting back together means a lot to him, and I'm so happy to have him back in my life," she says. "I'm just so glad that he made it. That we both made it. Life throws you all these things, but I look at him and I look at me and we became good people—we didn't let what had happened to us change us."

"We turned out pretty good," Don agrees.

"Something good happened out of something evil," she adds.

I asked Jeannine if she felt like she finally had closure—fifty-three years after her mother's death. Almost, she told me.

"Real closure would be to stand in front of Lolly and ask her, 'How could you not have known?'" she says. "But I don't know if that's ever going to happen, and maybe now I don't need it to happen."

BIBLIOGRAPHY

BOOKS

Andersen, Earl. *Hard Place to Do Time: The Story of Oakalla Prison, 1912–1991*. New Westminster, BC: Hillpointe Publishing, 1993.

Aronsen, Lawrence. *City of Love and Revolution: Vancouver in the Sixties*. Vancouver: New Star Books, 2010.

Barrett, Sylvia. *The Arsenic Milkshake and Other Mysteries Solved by Forensic Science*. Toronto: Doubleday Canada, 1994.

Blum, Deborah. *The Poisoner's Handbook: Murder and the Birth of Forensic Medicine in Jazz Age New York*. New York: Penguin Books, 2010.

Davis, Chuck. *The Chuck Davis History of Metropolitan Vancouver*. Pender Harbour, BC: Harbour Publishing, 2011.

———. *Top Dog! A History of CKNW, BC's Most Listened to Radio Station*. Vancouver: Canada Wide Magazines Ltd., 1993.

Duguid, Stephen. *Can Prisons Work? The Prisoner as Object and Subject in Modern Corrections*. Toronto: University of Toronto Press, 2000.

Hempel, Sandra. *The Inheritor's Powder: A Tale of Arsenic, Murder and the New Forensic Science*. New York: W.W. Norton & Company, 2013.

Kluckner, Michael. *Vancouver Remembered*. Vancouver: Whitecap Books, 2011.

Lazarus, Eve. *At Home with History: The Untold Secrets of Greater Vancouver's Heritage Homes*. Vancouver: Anvil Press, 2007.

McDonald, Glen, and John Kirkwood. *How Come I'm Dead?* Surrey, BC: Hancock House, 1985.

McNicoll, Susan. *British Columbia Murders: Notorious Cases and Unsolved Mysteries*. Calgary: Altitude Publishing, 2003.

Pattison, Jimmy, with Paul Grescoe. *Jimmy: An Autobiography*. Toronto: Seal Books, 1987.

Pauls, Naomi, and Charles Campbell. *The Georgia Straight: What the Hell Happened?* Vancouver: Douglas and McIntyre, 1997.

Phillips, Roderick. *Untying the Knot: A Short History of Divorce*. Cambridge, UK: Cambridge University Press, 1991.

Spaner, David. *Dreaming in the Rain: How Vancouver Became Hollywood North by Northwest*. Vancouver: Arsenal Pulp Press, 2003.

Webster, Jack. *Webster! An Autobiography by Jack Webster*. Vancouver: Douglas and McIntyre, 1990.

ARTICLES

Campbell, Robert. "Ladies and Escorts: Gender Segregation and Public Policy in British Columbia Beer Parlours, 1925–1945," *BC Studies* 105/106 (Spring/Summer 1995): 119–138.

Donaldson, Jesse. "'It's a Filthy, Perverted Paper': The History of the *Georgia Straight*," *Dependent*, July 13, 2010.

Harrison, Tom. "Series: History of Rock 'n' Roll in Vancouver: Part 5," *Province*, June 1, 1997.

Hawthorn, Tom. "Foncie Pulice 1914–2003: Vancouver's Karsh of the Concrete," *Globe and Mail*, March 25, 2003.

Lawrence, Grant. "Positively Fourth Avenue: The Rise and Fall of Canada's Hippie Mecca," *Westender*, October 19, 2016.

Mackie, John. "Vancouver Loved Going to Bed with Jack Cullen," *Vancouver Sun*, April 29, 2002.

Shapira, Allan, Gail Shapira, and Karen Ginsberg. "Lives Lived: Machelle (Chickie) Shapira, 78." *Globe and Mail*, March 20, 2015.

White, Kayce. "Ex-Coroner Proves There's Life after 26 Years of Death," *Vancouver Sun*, March 5, 1992.

DOCUMENTARY

Orr, George. *Talk! Vancouver's Fifty-Year Fascination with Grand Journalism and Instant Democracy*. Digital Artifact Production, 2017.

WEBSITES

"Beatles at Empire Stadium on CKNW." *RadioWest*. August 22, 2010. http://www.radiowest.ca/forum/viewtopic.php?f=19&t=8090.

Cristall, Gary. "27. East Is East and West Is West—Halifax, Ottawa, Toronto, Winnipeg, Regina, Calgary, Edmonton, Vancouver & Smaller Towns and Smaller Scenes." *A History of Folk Music in English Canada*. http://folkmusichistory.com/outline/27.shtml.

Frankel, M. ("Chickie"). "Jewel of the West (Beautiful B.C.)." *British Columbia Sheet Music.* http://bcsheetmusic.ca/htmpages/jewelof thewest.html.

Rosevere, Lee. "The Beatles Played Vancouver 50 Years Ago." CBC. August 22, 2014. http://www.cbc.ca/news/canada/british-columbia /the-beatles-played-vancouver-50-years-ago-1.2743085.

"Street Photography." *Vanalogue.* June 26, 2013. https://vanalogue .wordpress.com/2013/06/26/street-photography/.

"United Services Centre." *Vancouver As It Was: A Photo-Historical Journey.* August 10, 2014. https://vanasitwas.wordpress.com/2014/08/10 /united-services-centre/.

Verzuh, Ron. "Canada's A-Bomb Secret." *Canada's History.* July 14, 2015. http://www.canadashistory.ca/Explore/Science-Technology /Canada-s-A-Bomb-Secret.

PRIMARY SOURCES

CKNW tapes of Rene Castellani (1961–65)

Inquest for Donald Miller (September 25, 1962)

Inquest for Esther Castellani (December 1–3, 1965)

Inquest for the Willows Hotel fire (January 30, 1963) and police investigation report

Rene Castellani Supreme Court Appeal (September 25–October 6, 1967)

Taped interviews of Gloria Yusep by Susan McNicoll (2005 and 2006)

The Magic Pond CD

ACKNOWLEDGMENTS

Much gratitude goes to Susan McNicoll who wrote a chapter about the Castellani case for her 2003 book *British Columbia Murders*. Ill health prevented her from writing a book about the case, and she generously gave me her research and taped interviews.

Thanks to Dr Heather Burke, forensic psychologist, who took on the first read of the manuscript and was able to offer invaluable insights into the actions and behaviours of the people in this book. Special thanks to George Garrett, who worked at CKNW for more than forty years, knew all the players in the story, and generously shared his knowledge and opinions with me.

I'd also like to thank Vancouver filmmaker Colleen Hardwick, who loaned me the trial transcripts from Rene Castellani's appeal case and a few recordings of his broadcasts at CKNW—probably the only ones that still exist.

I am deeply grateful to the many experts that helped me with various aspects of this case—from the police investigation to a crash course in autopsy and the effects and detection of arsenic in the human body. Thank you to Mike Porteous, superintendent of the VPD's Investigation Division; Inspector Earl Andersen, VPD; Doug Lucas, retired director of the Ontario Centre of Forensic Sciences; Dr Elaine Willman, pathologist; Dr William Schreiber, former medical director of the Provincial Toxicology Centre; and professors Stephen Duguid, Roderick Phillips, Nikos Harris, and Neil Boyd for their help with different aspects of criminology and the law.

Thanks also to the friends of the Castellanis: Don and Debbie Miller, Rick and Mary Iaci, Gloria Cameron, Carol Baldwin, Lorraine Lavallee, and Sharon Wild for their memories.

Thank you to broadcasters Norm Grohmann, Bill Nelson, Barrie McMaster, John Plul, Bob Adshead, and Bob Singleton.

Thanks also to the Vancouver Police Museum and Archives for their awesomeness; BC Archives; Carolyn Soltau, news research librarian at the *Vancouver Sun* and *Province*; the Belshaw Gang, especially Aaron Chapman and Tom Carter; Bill Allman; Claire Dansereau; Rob Frith; Gary Cristall; Jerry Kruz; Christine Hagemoen; Brian Burch; Peter Nobes; and Steve Sweeney.

I'm especially grateful to the amazing team at Arsenal Pulp Press for taking me on for a third time. Thank you Brian Lam, Robert Ballantyne, Cynara Geissler, Oliver McPartlin, Shirarose Wilensky, Zoe Grams at ZG Communications, and all I can say is—thank god for my editor, Susan Safyan.

INDEX

PAGE NUMBERS IN *ITALICS* REFER TO PHOTOGRAPHS.

Photo: Rebecca Blissett

EVE LAZARUS is a journalist, crime historian, and author. Her passion for non-traditional history and a fascination with murder have led to six books of non-fiction, including the BC bestsellers *Blood, Sweat, and Fear: The Story of Inspector Vance, Vancouver's First Forensic Investigator*; *Cold Case Vancouver: The City's Most Baffling Unsolved Murders*; and *Sensational Vancouver*.

evelazarus.com